· S0-ADI-461

ACRL Publications in Librarianship no. 51

Constancy and Change in the Worklife of Research University Librarians

Rebecca Watson-Boone

DISCARD

Prof
024.70973
W337c

N.C. CENTRAL UNIVERSITY
SCHOOL OF LIBRARY & INFO. SCI.

Association of College and Research Libraries
A division of the American Library Association
Chicago 1998

Association of College and Research Libraries
Publications in Librarianship Editorial Board
John H. Budd, chair
Mark E. Cain
Margaret S. Dalton
Connie Vinita Dowell
Wanda K. Johnston
Ann E. Prentice
Sally C. Tseng
James F. Williams II

The paper used in this publication meets the minimum requirements of American National Standard for Information Sciences–Permanence of Paper for Printed Library Materials, ANSI Z39.48—1992.∞

Library of Congress Cataloging-in-Publication Data
Watson-Boone, Rebecca.
    Constancy and change in the worklife of research university
librarians / Rebecca Watson-Boone.
        p.   cm. -- (ACRL publications in librarianship ; no. 51)
    Includes bibliographical references and index.
    ISBN 0-8389-7984-X (alk. paper)
    1. Academic libraries--United States. I. Title. II. Series.
    Z675.U5W38 1998
    027.7'0973--dc21   98-26935

Copyright © 1998 by the American Library Association.
All rights reserved except those which may be granted by Sections 107 and 108 of the Copyright Revision Act of 1976.

Printed in the United States of America.

02 01 00 99 98   5 4 3 2 1

Table of Contents

Dedication

To MIRI-U librarians, whose rich descriptions of life at work broaden our understanding of academic librarianship.

To Peter, whose help and sharp eye are priceless.

All royalties will be paid to the Center for the Study of Information Professionals, Inc.

Introduction

This book is intended as a benchmark for what it is like to work as an academic librarian in a U. S. research university in the mid-1990s. It also allows the reader to consider changes occurring within the wider field of librarianship. The particular setting is a large, public, major research university affected by now-familiar budgetary constraints, along with increasing enrollments and public demands for educational reform. The librarians struggle with conflicts between limited resources, pressures for new technologies, and new and existing library services for users. As members of their library and university, they participate in the higher education and library changes going on around them, and ponder, evaluate, critique, and comment on pleasures and triumphs, on pains and confusions, and on the familiar and the new.

Such a benchmark is important because, although the professional literature of librarianship still focuses primarily on the library as a place, those discussions dealing with topics such as electronic technology and organizational change increasingly suggest changes in the very nature of the work that librarians do. Even the debate about what to call librarians ("cyberlibrarians," "information specialists," "knowledge workers," etc.) implies a reconsideration of what it is that makes a librarian a "librarian". If we can develop an understanding of the work of these particular academic librarians—and the meaning their work has for them—we can better grasp many of the changes currently affecting both librarians and libraries.

From Market to Service

The basic work-related change affecting librarianship rests on the shift from a manufacturing to a service economy that has been in progress for decades in the United States. More than half of the new jobs added to the

U. S. economy in the 1970s were in fields that offered buyers a service, such as banking or health care, rather than in construction or assembly line work. That kind of job shift continues to this day (Bills 1995). A service economy means moving from manufacturing work to more of what Mike Hales (1980) calls "thinkwork." It suggests Daniel Bell's knowledge-based post-industrialism, where "what counts is not raw muscle power, or energy, but information. The central person is the professional, for he [sic] is equipped by his education and training to provide the kinds of skill which are increasingly demanded" (Bell 1973, 127). Higher education and academic librarianship are part of the service economy and certainly exemplify the concept of thinkwork.

The Bell and Hales approaches offer a positive view of work change. This is the "up-skilling" notion that workers will be called upon to use brains more than brawn, and to accept increased personal responsibility for carrying out their jobs. Up-skilling proponents argue that new technologies automate more and more routine work, which frees workers to focus on higher levels of complexity and problem-solving. The nature of work in most service economy organizations is such that workers interact and cooperate with each other in accomplishing it. Thus, problem-solving means workers come to understand areas and tasks outside their own. They gain a larger picture of the organization and its goals, and see themselves as identified with more than a narrowly defined set of tasks. This up-skilling thesis is not new, having been cogently articulated by researchers such as Robert Blauner (1964), Larry Hirschhorn (1984), and Paul Adler (1984).

There are those, however, who believe that such an economic shift from manufacturing to service jobs results in just the opposite: an increase in "de-skilling." This view, as developed by Karl Marx (1867/1967) and expanded upon by Harry Braverman (1974), sees a proletarianized society where workers remain controlled by production processes. The de-skilling thesis is most effectively expressed in Braverman's *Labor and Monopoly Capital* (1974). Basically, he and others argue that jobs, and the skills they require, are continually being downgraded through that very routinization of work. As more tasks are automated, fewer workers are needed and those that are necessary spend more of their time responding to machine-driven commands.

Shoshana Zuboff (1988) postulates that new technologies can support either or both positions. Drawing upon contingency theory, she finds that automating routine work can realign remaining job elements in ways that free workers for problem-solving. It is the organization's culture and its managerial philosophy that tip the balance. It may also be that the mixture of specific skills required for a job is changing. Charles N. Darrah (1996, 8) cites Spenner (1988) and Cyert and Moery (1989), whose studies conclude that "there is no compelling evidence for either the massive upgrading or downgrading of skill requirements. [Instead,] changes in work are best viewed as requiring a 'reskilling' of the work force." Darrah goes on to note that "despite a vast and heterogeneous literature [on jobs and skills], relatively few studies . . . are based on direct observations of people at work or on interviews with workers." This book attempts to rectify that omission for one significant group of information professionals.

The Social–Psychological Approach

Although it is true that one of the classical themes in the sociology of work involves the effect of work on the individual (Vallas 1990), it is also true that the majority of studies emphasize the structural aspects of work. Centering a study on job content or design can lead to ignoring the people performing the work. And although psychology-of-work themes tend to focus on the worker, that is generally in order to change individuals' behaviors or attitudes so that they work more productively. In the service-based organization, such as an academic library, it is helpful to see work in a context of people, position, and purpose (Braude 1983). Work cannot be understood apart from organizational, group, and individual cultures and values. Conversely, workers cannot be understood apart from the tasks and jobs they undertake. To understand academic librarians' work, one must understand both the librarians and the work they do.

There are many things we already know from studies of work that are applicable in task and conceptual terms to academic librarians. For instance, from Kai Erikson (1990, 2), we know "that job conditions really do have an influence on personality . . . that the more autonomous and self-directed a person's work, the more positive its effects on personality [and] that these results hold for both men and women." Thoralf Qvale (1988, 218) summarizes many studies when he finds that people commonly expect (1) safety, security, income, a good social climate, and possibilities for using their skill, competence, and experience; (2) to learn in work, have influence, find a good fit between "work" and "nonwork"; and (3) to perform meaningful tasks. Lee Braude (1983, 176) notes that "workers *do* structure the parameters of their work to a far greater extent than is realized" [emphasis his]. And Rosabeth Moss Kanter (1990) points out that workers in professional fields can now be generally characterized as well educated, distrustful of authority in general and autocratic forms of management in particular, and desirous of participating in the design of both their work and work setting.

Librarians, Work, and Change

In discussing the dynamics of change, Qvale (1988, 211) says, "We are observing the *content* of work changing quite rapidly, we see the *context* of work and working changing, and we assume or think we observe the *concept* of work changing. Thus the meaning people attach to work and working would also change, we think" [emphases his]. Qvale reminds us that "what work and working means, ultimately is depend[ent] upon the evaluation from the workers themselves." This sentiment was echoed by the 1996 Library and Information Technology Association/Library Administration and Management Association National Conference planning committee when they set as their conference theme "Transforming Libraries: Leadership and Technology for the Information Age." Although emphasizing technological change, they solicited papers and presentations addressing a number of work and worklife concerns through the following program tracks descriptions:

• Strategic Environment—The Long-Range Perspective: Information services face a challenging environment of continuous change. Planners must look to innovative approaches to organization, management, and the delivery of services in order to realize the greatest potential use of information technology.

• Operational Environment—Managing the Near Future: The day-to-day service environment is increasingly reliant on sophisticated and complex technologies. Selecting and sustaining these technologies has created a new context for the management and delivery of services.

• Societal Roles—Determining How We Contribute: The nature of services and who is served is changing as a result of new technological capabilities. As new services evolve, organizational structures and human resource requirements are undergoing significant change as well.

• Collaboration—Defining New Partnerships: Partnering is a major factor in the delivery of services based on information technology. Users, vendors, and the providers of information services are working together in new ways to develop and deliver services.

It may be that a confluence of technological, economic, educational, and general societal changes is beginning to affect the very nature of the work that librarians do. By presenting the story of how 29 research university librarians see and respond to today's challenges, this book can serve as a reference point against which to assess subsequent work-related changes that occur in this kind of library.

The university that is home to these librarians is given the pseudonym of MIRI-U (Midwest Research I University). It is a multicampus institution with a decentralized library system composed of main, departmental, and subject-based library units. The librarians come from across the campus; none hold administrative positions. Chapter 1 begins with a broad overview of the concept and meaning of work itself, and concludes with a discussion of worklife and ways to understand how workers give meaning to what they do. Chapter 2 introduces the voices of the librarians at MIRI-U. From that chapter on, they help us see their world. The concluding chapter considers their postindustrial future. An appendix provides background on the librarians and describes the methodologies underlying the study on which this book is based.

1. Work

Until the late 1800s, most people typically asked someone they had just met Where are you from?; today, we ask What do you do? (Gross 1958). Work is a pivotal concern and the subject of many conversations. We frequently hear utterances such as: I'm spending more time at work than I used to; My work is changing—what will it be like in five years?; Am I going to be out of work? We spend a lot of time working and talking about work; it seems to dominate our lives. It provides a focus for self-identification, as well as a livelihood. It gives order to each day, and suggests personal and societal norms. We tend to talk about our work in ways that identify our field or profession, denote the use of certain tools or techniques, and reveal the kinds of commitments of self and time that we believe are important. However, as most scholars studying work note, it is not always easy to define the concept. What terminology should be used—that of economics? or politics? or religion? Does your gender, race, age, and ethnicity make a difference in how you define and give meaning to "work" (see Braverman 1974 and Burawoy 1979)? Is work only that for which you are paid? Is it manipulation of one person by another, as in the phrase "to hire someone to work"? Is work something that denotes "being responsible"? If you like and enjoy what you are doing, can that activity be work—perhaps it is "play"? Can work be fun?

Like most concepts, work has no absolute or intrinsic meaning; it is subject to interpretations given by language, culture, time, and place (Mills 1951; Brief and Nord 1990; du Gay 1996). Classical Greeks considered work unworthy—slaves worked so that citizens could spend their time

1

with the more important results that came from such activity. In the Middle Ages, people associated work with the creation of wealth and with altering the natural world to serve human needs. During the Reformation, Luther argued that all people must work at whatever God calls them to do. "Calling" denoted acceptance, action, and work as fulfilling. Calvin also believed that everyone must work—rich and poor alike—because it is God's will. It was considered good to be successful in one's work, which suggested the idea of "work for work's sake," along with notions of self-discipline and personal achievement (Applebaum 1992).

Gradually, this religion-based work ethic shifted toward that of a craft ethic and then a capitalistic ethic, where hard work and thrift were for oneself rather than for God. During the Industrial Revolution, factory production meant moving large numbers of workers from diverse home sites to a single location and imposing standardized discipline. Workers attempted to hold on to notions of self-reliance, individualism and craft skill, but by the nineteenth century, growing emphasis on mechanistic processes and company needs subordinated many values associated with individual skills. As the age of scientific management made work tasks more explicit, routinized, and controlled, craft workers lost many unique aspects of their skills (Zuboff 1988).

Conflict between the idea of work as discipline and work as a creative, individual act presented mid-nineteenth-century Americans with a dilemma: Discipline reinforced a strict work ethic, but technological and commercial innovation appeared possible only under conditions of personal creativity, spontaneity, and self-expression. Although people increasingly took jobs that separated them from their homes and made them dependent on others, such work also promised upward mobility through economic and social rewards (Rodgers 1978; Howard 1995b). In the twentieth century, work has become perhaps the most important single factor in status and self-respect for the individual. The kind of work performed, along with choice of occupation and work setting, does appear to affect self-esteem, personal identity, and the meanings and values we associate with American life (Applebaum 1992).

Today, the average dictionary may provide as many as fifty definitions for work "without claiming to cover all [those] developed in various disciplines such as physics, theology, philosophy, sociology, anthropology, economics, [and] psychology" (Ruiz Quintanilla and

Wilpert 1988, 6-7). However, common to many definitions is the underlying notion that work is some kind of purposeful activity. To biologists, it involves muscular movement. Industrial psychologists see work as a set of "tasks" containing identifiable steps or parts. Sociologists view it as centered on relationships, with individuals performing activities that achieve objectives usually set by others (Gross 1958). Almost everyone also assumes there is an economic rationale for work. The Meaning of Working International Research Team (MOW IRT) believes this connection between work and paid employment arose because the institutionalization of working occurred within the Industrial Revolution (1987). As work moved away from family or home context, it became redefined as a market activity that is "purchased." Indeed, a 1987 MOW IRT eight country study of 15,000 workers of various occupations, genders, and ages found that the great majority of workers now equate "my work" and "my job" with a set of tasks for which they are paid and which they undertake to satisfy a wide variety of perceived needs that generally require the exchange of money.

Professional Work

Although there is still debate about what qualifies an occupation to be defined as "professional," there is general agreement on characteristics that describe professional work. In the United States, researchers such as Talcott Parsons, Everett C. Hughes, Harold L. Wilensky, William J. Goode, and Eliot Freidson labored long to identify similarities and differences between professions and other occupations. Within the past decade, Samuel Haber (1991) and Andrew Abbott (1988) have continued the study of professions as a concept and in terms of specific fields. The professions most frequently studied are medicine, law, nursing, and K–12 teaching. There are also publications about specific groups of workers that cross professional-occupational lines, from C. Wright Mills's 1951 *White Collar: The American Middle Classes* to Paula J. Dubeck and Kathryn Borman's 1996 *Women and Work: A Handbook*. Within librarianship, we have examples such as Dee Garrison's 1979 *Apostles of Culture: The Public Librarian and American Society, 1876–1920*, Orvin Lee Shiflett's 1981 *Origins of American Academic Librarianship*, and Roma M. Harris's 1992 *Librarianship: The Erosion of a Woman's Profession*. Among those writing about professions, there has been a general shift away from focusing on a group's role in holding society together and toward issues of domain, conflict, and power (Freidson 1994).

Although not denying differences between various professions, such research does suggest some common characteristics of professional work. There is its seemingly contradictory quality: Altruism with its focus on service to and for others is present but so is self-interested behavior on the part of professional workers. Professional work entails concern about autonomy and authority in the conduct of tasks and jobs. It bespeaks monopolistic privilege and jurisdictional rights of one profession's type of work over that of another profession. Professional work includes the concept of control over clients. Yet, although individuals carry out the actual work, the profession itself exerts control over those individuals through the imposition of certain requirements for education, behavior, belief, and standards of practice.

Work is conceived of as a whole, rather than as piece work; compensation is by annual salary, not hourly wage. Professionals of all kinds generally believe the worth of their work is not appropriately respected or rewarded. This concern appears tied to professionals' belief that those outside the specific profession do not understand the very nature of its work. Yet across professions, work is seen as creative and complex in nature, and as requiring degrees of independent judgment. Although each profession makes jealous distinctions on the degree of intelligence required to perform its specific activities, members of each field generally believe professional work necessarily requires a high degree of intellect. Abstract and practical knowledge are used in work activities, with the former more highly prized. Tasks requiring certain knowledges are bundled together into specifically designed jobs. The greater the required abstract knowledge, the higher the rank and salary; individuals holding such positions tend to have more autonomy, formal authority, and personal power. Tasks that involve identifying, reasoning about, and acting upon problems that belong to a specific profession's domain epitomize professional work (Abbott 1988).

Those engaged in this kind of work can carry it around in their heads because much of it is "thinkwork" (Hales 1980). Because of its mental nature, beginning with the education underlying it and the worker's commitment to both a profession and the services associated with it, professional work tends to have strong significance or "centrality" for the worker.

The Meaning of Working

When people talk about the meaning of working, generally they speak from a perspective drawn from the psychology of work, the sociology of work, or from social psychology. Although this book takes the latter point of view, it is helpful to briefly review all three lines of thought.

Psychologists study how the individual senses, perceives, feels, thinks, and acts; the focus is on the individual. Regardless of the school of thought (such as Gestalt theory, learning theory, psychoanalysis, behaviorism), the aim is to account for different aspects of the behavior of individuals (Merton 1982). Work psychologists endeavor to identify and resolve psychological problems that arise within the working environment. An outgrowth of industrial/organizational psychology (I/O), the psychology of work focuses on work in terms of the actions and reactions of an individual to activities taking place within the workplace and within that worker's own job. The field's theoretical underpinnings are supported by Taylor's scientific management endeavors and the Hawthorne studies (see Applebaum 1992: 456–457), Hackman and Oldham (1980), and, more recently, by the MOW International Research Team (1987).

The psychology of work incorporates personnel and organizational specialties. Personnel psychology examines the role of individual differences and deals with drawing up position descriptions, recruiting and selecting new hires, and developing and reviewing promotion and termination criteria. Matching the right individual to the work to be performed is crucial to satisfying both an individual's and an organization's needs. Organizational psychology studies the impact of groups and other social influences on the individual worker's role-related feelings and behaviors. Organizational psychology seeks to identify behavioral factors relating to issues such as job satisfaction, morale, motivation, and conflict resolution. Both specialties are concerned with how individuals can be motivated to carry out the needs of the organization (de Cock 1986). The effects of change and expectation on performance, feelings that accompany participation in decision-making, reaction to the division of labor between professionals and other staff members, motives behind choice of hours of work, even the question of how much autonomy an individual should have in carrying out his or her job—all are psychology of work issues. Within librarianship, two current endeavors would be studying attitudes, reactions, and behaviors of librarians vis-à-vis electronic technologies, and developing mechanisms to ensure that decreasing resources and increasing user demands do not unduly lower librarian morale and productivity.

From a psychological perspective, the meaning that work has for individual librarians is found by studying their abilities, interests, aptitudes, and personality traits. The resulting characteristics can then be used to infer behavior patterns and to predict how librarians will react to situations in their place of work.

Sociologists study group processes and group behaviors. Here, the focus is on characterizing the attributes, processes, structures, and functions of the environments in which individuals find themselves:

> What the psychologist seeks to discover systematically about individuals, provisionally abstracted from their environments, the sociologist seeks to discover systematically about the environments, abstracted temporarily from the particular individuals in them. Just as psychologists seek to identify the significant attributes of individuals, so sociologists seek to identify significant attributes of social and cultural environments (Merton 1982, 169).

Sociologists who study work look at group roles and behaviors within, on, and in reaction to the work environment. Significant contributions have been made by Emile Durkheim, Max Weber, the University of Chicago school of thought under Everett C. Hughes, and more recent thinkers including C. Wright Mills and Erving Goffman. Hughes's "work drama" concept is often used to characterize the study of interactions between people while at their place of work. Making "sense" of work as a social phenomenon is important to the sociological perspective.

Within librarianship, questions would include: What is a library's "culture"? How has its organizational structure evolved and changed? What are the social values, norms, rules, and controls that exist within it? How do librarians learn what is required in order to become socialized—to become a "member" of the group—in a particular library? Indeed, what are the groups that exist; are they bound by department, work role, seniority? Although these topics range from abstract to concrete, they are studied as structural elements of the environment in which librarians find themselves. From a sociological perspective, the meaning of work carries an environmental or organizational connotation in that members of an occupation are seen as coming together for individual and social survival, usually with some sort of benefit accruing to those involved (Braude 1983). The meaning that work has for individual librarians is found by studying interactions and relationships between librarians and their library, as well as between them and larger entities such as their university. The world of the librarian while at work in a library, the effect of structural reorganization on librarywide communication patterns, and what happens when the number of a library's managers is reduced or when librarians are organized into teams rather than departments are questions of interest to sociologists of work.

Social psychology brings together strands from both sociology and psychology. This approach seeks to relate "the variability of individuals and the variability of the social environment" by understanding and explaining how the "thought, feeling, and behavior of individuals are influenced by the actual, imagined, or implied presence of others" (Merton 1982, 170; Vander Zanden 1987, 33). This kind of researcher finds it as difficult to study the individual and ignore the setting as to study the setting and ignore the individual. Each aspect is seen as having a profound effect on the other. Thus, the social psychology of work concerns matters such as group membership, motivation, personality development, and social interaction (Strauss 1959). Drawing on concepts from both the psychology and the sociology of work, the social-psychological domain ranges from, for example, studying personal beliefs and the idea of institutional culture, to considering the individual's need for conformity and obedience to authority in light of a seemingly equal desire for personal autonomy in doing one's job. Attitudes and factors underlying attitudinal change bring both the individual and the environment into consideration. For example, the notion that a librarian works more purposively when in the presence of others engaged in the same activity typifies an issue with a social-psychological base.

Studying work through this combined approach includes considering individual social behaviors such as social perceptions and attributions, communication and language, socialization and development, role identity and the self, attitudes and attitudinal change. It includes interpersonal social behavior, such as norms, roles, territoriality, altruism and helping behavior, as well as aggression and conflict. Finally, such an approach considers social behavior within and across groups, with "groups" defined by a range of characteristics such as position, gender, race/ethnicity, along with primary and secondary reference groups and memberships. In academic librarianship, an example of the last concept is seen in studies of how librarians have attempted to pattern themselves after disciplinary faculty and the degree to which they believe they have or have not succeeded.

What Is Real?

What people define as reality is based on continuing personal negotiation (social interaction) as they continually define and redefine their own realities. A complete definition of work therefore requires a consideration of the fact that work is what we define it to be. Work is thus a socially constructed phenomenon as well as an objective activity (Hall 1986, 13).

The MOW IRT (1987, 212) eight-country study confirmed Hall's observation by finding that "not only do people assign many meanings to working, but the patterning [gestalt of experience and interpretation] of those meanings also varies." In other words, "meanings vary as jobs vary and as people vary" (Friedmann and Havighurst 1954, 15). An example: In their study of the significance that work and retirement had for steelworkers, coal miners, salespersons, skilled craftsmen, and physicians, Eugene A. Friedmann and Robert J. Havighurst (1954) found that all but the physicians generally saw their work as having no other meaning than that of earning money. Only physicians, the sole professional group, gave high value to the work-meaning phrase "service to others" and described their activities as "nice work."

Individuals apply values and preferences to work tasks and jobs as part of interacting with those activities. Features or properties ascribed to work vary as individuals use job content and context terms to explain, give meaning to, and represent those activities and the settings in which they take place. The values and preferences a librarian gives to an activity or a work situation become part of his or her own construction of a workplace reality. As librarians go about their work over time, they construct reality from and through their own thoughts and actions. Everyday worklife begins to seem "ordered" with phenomena integrated into patterns librarians share with each other. As they talk and work together, a professional language (a jargon), a culture, and shared meanings become established (Berger and Luckmann 1966; MOW IRT 1987).

One way to discern what is real for a group is to identify how central work is for its members. *Work centrality* is the extent to which a person defines him- or herself through work and expresses a commitment to working (MOW IRT 1987). The centrality concept refers to the value, rather than the content, of outcomes available at work in comparison to those available or sought from other facets of life (Roberson 1990). This approach to identifying work meaning was first studied by Dubin (1956), and the MOW IRT (1987) placed this concept at the heart of one current psychological model of the meaning of work. Individuals who have a strong sense of work as central to their lives put in longer hours, are very satisfied with their occupation, rationalize low pay as the "price" for doing something they love, and generally believe in doing their duty more than in gaining specific rights. They convey a sense of job enjoyment. The MOW IRT researchers have found that workers across country, occupation, gender, and age who feel an obligation to their organization or to society score high in terms of work as central in their lives. Conversely, workers who stress entitlement to certain rights from their organization or society score low and generally stress the economic benefits of work over job enjoyment.

A narrower way to discern the meaning work has for a group is to identify how satisfied members of it are with their jobs. Jeylan T. Mortimer (1979) suggests that having autonomy and responsibility stimulate involvement with work and, especially when experienced early in a work career, lead to a self-directed orientation that contributes to both job satisfaction and work centrality. The level of satisfaction with one's overall work affects the specifics of the tasks being carried out. Satisfaction may result from extrinsic or intrinsic features of the overall job, or from some combination of the two. *Extrinsic features* center on job tasks, but may include occupational as well as organizational characteristics. *Intrinsic features* focus on the attributes of the worker including psychological motivators inherent in the work experience, as well as education, gender, race, and other social characteristics (Mortimer 1979). If work forms a major activity for librarians, then what that work is—and whether they like it—becomes important.

Do librarians have a strong sense of work centrality that fits the MOW IRT model of working long hours and viewing work positively? Do librarians value outcomes such as job responsibility, personal growth, and usefulness of the organization's products or services? Or are librarians more like workers with low centrality scores: valuing such things as time for personal needs, knowing tasks in advance, and socializing while working? Perhaps librarians have multiple preferred outcomes for their work. That is, they may value some ratio of both intrinsic and extrinsic rewards for their work.

As individual librarians work together, tasks, events, and jobs gradually become integrated into objectified, shared-meaning patterns exhibiting a set of common values and preferences that include expressions of work centrality and job satisfaction. Over time, differences among group members diminish in importance or at least are tolerated and accepted as understandable to almost everyone in the group. Work life appears structured in terms of the familiar, the known, the routine, and eventually the taken-for-granted. Individuals do not need to define each situation anew, step by step: "If one says, 'This is how these things are done' often enough, one believes it oneself"—and sees it as "real" and as "common knowledge" (Berger and Luckmann 1966, 60; Ford 1975). Shared definitions and judgments come together to constitute a work—and work life—reality for librarians.

2. "Tell Me What You Do"

Like most people, MIRI-U librarians come into their formal positions with a job description and expectations.[1] Soon, they begin to nudge some tasks one way and others another way, gradually coming to find a group that they particularly enjoy. According to Braude (1983), this kind of redefining of a job is a natural part of learning a work role. Taking on a new position or set of tasks includes being exposed to new ideas and behaviors. It means confirming some expectations while putting others aside. Changes in expectation and behavior result in development of a new or revised mental model one's work and of one's personal work identity: "New ideas mean that the individual is not who he [sic] was. And when that person learns to see himself in new ways, such that he can apply new labels to himself and his behavior, he has changed his identity" (p. 166).

The identity individuals create for themselves at work begins with a mental map of what they believe are job boundaries and contours. Philip N. Johnson-Laird (1983, 5) notes that "to understand a phenomenon is to have a working model of it." Such a map is personal and idiosyncratic, and it is usually a mixture of objective knowledge and subjective perceptions about the work the individual will be doing. As people gain experience with their work, the map expands and is refined. It grows to contain impressions of self and colleagues, of tasks that are valued and devalued, of institution and profession (Singleton 1989). Ultimately, as it fills with meaning, each person's mental map represents an ever-changing summary of their work and their sense of self while at work.

11

The result of mental mapping is an expanded sense of work and creation of a work identity. The result of redefining a job is the identification of a cluster of tasks that most closely corresponds to our expression of our work identity. At MIRI-U, librarians appear to divide their activities into primary and secondary clusters.[2] Primary work is where the librarians prefer to spend their time; this is their favorite work, and it expresses their work identities. Secondary work is filled with "the other things I have to do." When talking about what they do, MIRI-U librarians initially list various tasks and jobs, responding in position description fashion. Quickly, however, they move to elaborate on a select few activities that comprise their primary work. MIRI-U librarians are internally motivated to do primary work. They have knowledge of its needs and the results of carrying it out. They feel responsibility for those results. They experience that cluster of tasks as meaningful, as something that "counts" in their own system of values (Hackman and Oldham 1980). Primary work is that set of tasks and activities upon which a librarian spends the greatest amount of time or by which a librarian defines her or himself. There are three clusters of primary work and one of quasi-primary work that dominate MIRI-U librarians' perception of their work and work lives:

- Collection work
- Catalog work
- Reference work
- Learning–teaching–training work

The first three are primary clusters and are familiar to all information professionals. Librarians routinely engage in the fourth but consider it secondary work. For a small number of academic librarians, this latter cluster is beginning to take on characteristics of primary work.

Collection Work

Over the past one hundred years, this kind of library work has changed from entailing intimate involvement in the details of selection and review of each new title to focusing on broad conceptual mapping of subject knowledges (Tuttle 1976). At MIRI-U, *collection work* refers to selection and maintenance of the library's holdings, including decisions regarding retention and preservation of material. A range of librarians perform this work—from those in reference areas to subject bibliographers to librarians in subject libraries.

Selection. Librarians "select" material when they identify and obtain items they judge helpful for library users[3] or for adding definition to a subject area under development. An approval plan covers most of the general stack collections and a portion of the subject libraries. MIRI-U selectors work with this plan in three ways. First, they develop profiles representing specific subject areas, including topics, languages, and publication years or time periods reflecting the areas. Publishers included in the plan automatically send new materials that match such profiles. Second, librarians review incoming materials on a weekly basis to determine whether the profiles established for specific subject fields are bringing in relevant publications. And third, they revise profiles to match changes in a field's literature and/or in the focus of related departments on campus.

To identify individual titles not covered by an approval plan, librarians use various secondary sources: society publication lists, notification slips sent by publishers and jobbers, catalogs of holdings of similar collections in other libraries, donated material, and specific items recommended by disciplinary faculty. Referring to her internationally recognized subject library, Peg reports that "many of our offers . . . come by fax [or] by letter." In his scientific subject area, Galen frequently finds such secondary sources are "kind of weird. A lot of them are not mainline publishers [but] tiny little societies or state surveys. A lot of them won't allow for standing orders, and so I spend a lot of time going through catalogs and making phone calls." Bob speaks for many librarians when he summarizes the process:

> You look at the material coming in [on approval], and if it is acceptable . . . your selection is then brought down to material that is requested by faculty, that doesn't fall into a regular publisher, or it's material that you locate either in the foreign publishing or in some of the smaller organizations around the United States. . . . [It] turns into a lot of looking through stuff, looking for things that aren't going to come in on a plan.

For these librarians, collection work starts with identifying and selecting a core of materials through an approval plan process, and continues by adding enriching materials reflecting either developments in the field, or needs of users, or depth for the subject.

For those in archival collections, selection is somewhat different. Their core materials may be those received from, or associated with, an organization, individual, or institution. Mark explains that:

> You start with the formal core records . . . and then you start to see the holes in that. You have [for example] the board minutes, the account budget records for the year, but there's something missing here about the essence of this thing. . . . We'll go after personal papers of individual leaders in an organization whose records we have.

Regardless of their unit's focus, as a group, MIRI-U selectors agree that this type of work means "trying to build a collection that will serve everybody . . . that will have some lasting benefit. So there's a certain core that I have to collect that may not have a person that belongs to it, but it has to be [here] anyway" (Galen).

Part of collection work is supporting the academic teaching and research missions of the university. Librarians with faculty department liaison responsibilities develop their understanding of faculty needs by meeting on a periodic basis with designated faculty-library representatives or advisory committees; reading departmental newsletters and notices to detect trends in faculty interest; attending colloquia and departmental meetings to better grasp faculty research areas and concerns; surveying faculty to assess interests; and even arranging to pick up mail at the departmental mail counter "where I can connect with them" (Karen). These activities help selectors discern whether new or changed foci are developing, so "I can structure what I'm doing to reflect that change" (Galen). Through such encounters librarians also anticipate class needs, for at MIRI-U one ideal of collection work is "to have here the materials the students and faculty need before they [know] about most of them" (Elizabeth).

Librarians learn how to select materials by spending as much time as possible with their subject areas. Peg says, "As soon as I really kind of knew the collection, I was given responsibility for acquisitions." And to this day, she points out, "The first thing is what is it and how does it fit into our scope? . . . [Items] would not be here if they were not subject related." Galen, who spends about 30 percent of his time on collection work, learned by "watching the collection that had been built up and trying to sense the direction that it was going." He also finds that in "doing reference, helping people that need help, you develop a sense of what [they] are using or not using." Some selectors conduct studies of the online catalog to determine frequency of use in their subject fields. Others enroll in courses to better understand a field for which they have taken responsibility. In commenting on how an intern learned selection, Elizabeth acknowledges, "I had forgotten what a long time it takes to get into being comfortable making decisions about individual books and to think of a book as it fits into a context of other books." Peg adds, "It's experience basically," regardless of the format or subject of materials.

Time is required to gain such experience. And time involvement increases as purchasing budgets shrink: More time must be spent determining the value of individual titles versus their cost. During the 1960s, when library budgets and the amount of information being published increased, collection librarians expanded efforts to buy materials on a wide variety of topics. But the lean budget years since then, along with decreases in the number of copies published of each new title and the length of time it is available for purchase, have meant collection librarians now must do more with both less money and less time (Weber 1976; Loe 1986; Branin 1991). For example, the quickness with which materials go out of print means librarians cannot afford to let catalogs and other collection work sources "pile up." Elizabeth sets a goal of reviewing a specific number of selection tools each day to stay up with some of her areas:

> But I'm still behind. I should do something else before the day ends in order to keep up with the year's output as I view it through a sort of pattern I have made of reviewing tools, announcement tools, gathering plans—a sort of package I have put together that gives me confidence that I'm looking at everything I need to look at. So looking at 2.5 selection tools per day is my constant.

Collection work is primary work for some librarians, secondary work for others. Those who do selection from a base in reference services or subject libraries view this type of work as one of several tasks they do and, in general, give it secondary preference to other activities. Galen is typical of those who find other activities more enjoyable: "I don't think I'd miss the collection development probably" if one of his tasks had to cease. Fran supports that, reflecting "I'm not sure that it's needed for [my] particular department in any level more than the level that I'm doing." However, for those librarians called "subject bibliographers," collection work is clearly their primary work.

Subject Bibliography. In the 1980s, MIRI-U stopped classifying librarians as faculty. In the library, the director at the time created a Subject Bibliography Unit to support primarily acquisitions/collection and reference librarians who wished to maintain their faculty standing. Currently, membership in this unit includes some selectors who split their work between it and a reference department, and who prefer tasks more strongly associated with reference work. It also includes those for whom collection work is the dominant activity. MIRI-U librarians view these latter individuals as "specialists in their given areas. . . . They may have a fairly limited, narrow range . . . , but they are very deep in [their] area" (Nancy).

Called subject bibliographers by themselves and others, these librarians see collection work as intense, and as having many aspects. Rose describes it as "really a way of life." Elizabeth agrees, defining a subject bibliographer as one who "carves up the world and says, 'I will do this.'" Most believe they have more autonomy than other librarians. They feel ownership over discrete subject areas reflected in the library's holdings. Judith defines her work as being "responsible for all of the library collections in [my] fields. Both new material coming in, also older material, managing the collection, preservation decisions, the whole—, anything having to do with that." Nancy, who is not a subject bibliographer, calls such work "a very heavy responsibility."

Subject bibliographers see themselves as more than selectors. They work closely with faculty in related departments. They provide specialized instruction and reference service primarily to graduate students and upper-division undergraduates. More so than part-time selectors, they see their disciplinary departments as integral parts of their work world. As specialists in given fields, subject bibliographers see this work as anticipating the teaching, research, and learning needs of current and future faculty and students. Beyond that, they seek continuous development and refinement of their own particular vision of each field's scope and definition. In terms of format, books and journals receive greatest attention; concern for electronic and other nonprint materials depends on the subject areas involved.

Speaking for several bibliographers, Elizabeth believes in "standing with one foot in the discipline and with one foot in the trade"—meaning she also needs to understand the work of acquisitions, accounting, technical processing, online systems, and reference. Bob sees this as knowing "everything about your system," yet Judith finds that, for the most part, such librarians "enjoy working alone. . . . We tend to be very sort of fragmented and to go our own way and are difficult to administer, and sort of uppity." She adds that because each bibliographer has an individual office, "our working arrangement has contributed to that." Indeed, working in a generally solitary fashion contributes to what Michele calls doing "very one-on-one, high-end-of-the-scale" work.

The health and welfare of their subject areas is as important to subject bibliographers as is supporting user needs. They emphasize their fields first almost as organisms that live on their own, and second as material in support of users. More than any others, these values explain why subject bibliographers give strong positive value to providing advanced reference service related to their subject area, and strong negative value to providing general reference or information desk support. This latter work would not relate to their fields; thus it is outside their perception or definition of themselves and their work.

Catalog Work

The concept of catalog work encompasses bibliographic and authority control tasks. This work allows for development, maintenance, and use of predominantly bibliographic files. Regardless of physical format or arrangement of entries, such catalogs consist of records representing items in one or more libraries and carry information about where those items can be found (Chan 1994). MIRI-U librarians see such files as essential finding aids for anyone wishing to obtain information from a library. Although some things can indeed be found by random chance, serendipity, or previous experience, librarians stress clarity and order over guesswork and chaos. As a resource combining description and location, catalogs serve to narrow users' queries to the point of identifying appropriate materials with a higher probability than would occur through random chance. A catalog symbolizes order.

At MIRI-U, efforts continue to catalog all material within the library system regardless of physical location or format: books, serials, AV, photographs, manuscripts, correspondence, association, and society ephemera. Perhaps the only items not yet regularly included are computer disk and tape files. Presently, there is a variety of "library catalogs." When MIRI-U librarians talk about or consult "the catalog," they generally mean the one most available to their library users: MIRIUCAT. It contains records of materials held across the library system, on open and closed stack shelving, in basic service areas and subject libraries; it connects with the Internet to make available the catalogs of other libraries. It is automated, and catalog librarians order, arrange, and enhance it according to both national rules/standards and local practices. The records for holdings of MIRI-U subject libraries not yet found in the online catalog are contained in on-site catalogs. In these latter locations, librarians distinguish between their local catalog ("our catalog") and MIRIUCAT ("the library's catalog"). Elaine compares hers with MIRIUCAT by saying:

> I suppose if we're going to look at it from a professional cataloger's standpoint, it isn't as elaborate. . . . We've created a reference catalog rather than a bibliographic catalog, so it's for—, it's to enable us to find things. We've got our own classification scheme. And then we do bend the subject rules to a certain extent because we need to get at certain things that are very peculiar [which] might not be allowable in the LC scheme of things.

Catalogs are of unique concern to those charged with their construction, enhancement, revision, and maintenance. At MIRI-U, two kinds of librarians have cataloging responsibilities: those for whom it is primary work (hereafter called catalogers) and those in subject libraries for whom it is balanced with other tasks (subject library catalogers). Those connected with catalog work believe "the main thing is to make sure that this material is out front, and [users] can find it" (Elaine). Catalogers tend to speak in terms of providing access to the array of material in the library system and to do this for a generalized user collective. Subject library catalogers speak of bringing their particular holdings out of "isolation" and to the attention of specific kinds of users.

Both kinds of catalogers view catalogs as dynamic. Catalogs grow, as when one massive project culminated with Lynne "waking up one morning and two hundred thousand [new] cataloguing records were in the catalog." They also change to reflect the world, as well as advances in the field. As Andy notes, "The world changes—the picture that everyone carries around of the world changes, and the catalog has to change with it. And at the same time, there are changes in the rules and formats which, for the most part, enable us to analyze things more [and more] finely."

Bibliographic Cataloging. Cataloging tasks include descriptive and subject cataloging of materials in specific subject areas or formats; supervising staff and students; enhancing records to include reference tool contents; maintaining records and files; resolving catalog-related problems; setting and coordinating cataloging policies; carrying out catalog conversion projects; and serving on catalog-related committees. The fundamental value of this work is succinctly expressed by Brooke: "If it weren't for us, nobody would have access to anything." Through use of standards, rules, and interpretations, catalogers determine what and how information will be presented to users. Basically, they do information control work.

Catalog work focuses on records: their construction, their details, their representation of matching items at hand. Thus, one characteristic of this work is that it is an active, decision-making process. It encompasses "physical description of information resources so that they can be identified usefully and uniquely, [with the] assignment and formulation of access points to those resources based on appearance, publishing pattern and history, and intellectual responsibility for the work" (Hill 1994, 45).

Another characteristic is that catalogers work alone or in close physical proximity to a few cataloging colleagues. Cataloging comes to those who do this work: It is a set of activities done in a centralized location. MIRI-U librarians do not catalog at the online catalog or in library stacks. And although catalog work can, and frequently does, involve field research into reference areas, open stacks, and subject libraries, it is characterized by materials and technologies localized within physical reach of these librarians. This work is carried out at one's desk in one's office or department—whether that is the central department in MIRI-U library's Humanities & Social Sciences (HSS) building or in one of the other library facilities.

To describe an item's physical characteristics and decide its bibliographic access points, MIRI-U catalogers use codes, rules, and interpretations set forth in various editions and publications related to the *Anglo-American Cataloging Rules*, machine-readable formats, a variety of national libraries, and various international bodies. Subject analysis of an item's content comes from the *Library of Congress Subject Headings* list and/or from specialized lists such as *Medical Subject Headings*. Whether discussing catalogs or Internet search engines, MIRI-U librarians place high value on the consistency provided by use of standards and established rules. They also agree that the more specialized the material, the more difficult it is to apply other than local standards. Elaine finds that cataloging manuscripts in a subject collection (for example) means "you're probably using twenty to thirty subject headings and added entries, whereas in a book, you feel you're splurging if you have five or six." Yet catalogers note there are also negative values associated with moving away from established national rules and standards. For instance, in one local situation, Margaret "thought all they needed was something to hang a receipt record on. So I thought sort of anything I could find in RLIN [Research Libraries Information Network] would do. . . . Of course, when the bar coding and all that came along and they needed it for circulation, then of course the records had to be very accurate." Thus, although MIRI-U catalogers do interpret rules for local conditions, they do so with some reluctance. Too many times, they have experienced the systematic, time-consuming, and thorough recataloging a local catalog requires when it becomes part of MIRIUCAT, which is maintained at the level of national standards.

Authority Control. This activity is defined as using specific records and files to:

> control the form and definition of headings and multiply access to them. . . . Verifying a heading in an authority file marks the beginning of true authority work, while establish-

ing and managing headings with authority records in an
authority file becomes the central task of [this work]. . . .
The shared nature of cataloging explains the need for authority control to standardize headings [as] catalogers . . .
find that individuals cannot be relied on to use the same terms
for their headings and searches. The authority file was developed to record and authorize the forms of headings used in a
library's bibliographic records (Hearn 1994, 86).

Both catalogers and authority control librarians work with records.
However, where catalogers begin with the item to create the record, authority control librarians begin with the subsequent record and go to an
item only to determine if the names associated with it are being used
correctly and consistently. Where catalogers live on the database development side of catalog work, authority librarians live on the database management side.

Andy sees authority control work as dealing with a "higher level of
generality in the catalog—not so much with individual books, but more
with the collocating points in the catalog." His goal is "that somebody
who looks under a name will get to the proper name they should look
under, and they will find everything the library has there." And that, he
adds, "makes sense to people." As Arthur T. Hamlin (1981, 204) points
out, "the effort expended on rules [is] enormous. [Yet] behind all this is
the basic conflict between the broad concept of cataloging as an art in
which the practitioner exercises considerable judgment and cataloging as
a science with a rule to cover every possible need." Such a combination of
rule-constructing and rule-applying, especially in an online catalog environment, is very pleasurable to Andy:

I think that rules are essential. I like the rules. I like rule-
governed activities. I studied Latin and Greek because they
have grammar and conjugation rules and all that. I like playing games because they have rules. And I like authority work
because there's lots of rules.

Part of his work is to help "show how behind the rule there is a
principle. There is a rational purpose that [anyone] can understand."

Authority control work means bringing catalogers and users to the point where they can "see both the specific rule and the larger context of consequences and connections and underlying purposes that make the rule rational" (Andy). Rules, rationality, and control are frequent words in Andy's conversation and work. Because he does not want "people having to guess which form of the name has been used in the catalog," he sees his work as fundamentally "picking a term that will be used as a heading, providing references from the alternatives that weren't used, and establishing relationships between related terms."

Authority control tasks include supervising the work of support staff; correcting headings in the MIRIUCAT database; establishing authority records; training colleagues and staff in authority-related aspects of MIRIUCAT; creating new authority records and adding them to the national file via the Library of Congress's National Coordinated Cataloging Operations (NACO) program; and "sit[ting] on various committees and stuff like that." Such librarians see high positive value and significance in this very time-consuming and detail-based kind of catalog work. Establishing an authority record is a meandering, uncharted process of consulting reference sources and existing rules and their interpretations, reviewing precedent, and defining the essence of an entity at hand. Andy offers an illustration:

> I've currently got a stack of material on my desk about a medieval French Chanson de Geste, and it is part of an epic cycle referred to as "The Old French . . . (something) Cycle." But parts of it may be parts of something else, and it's not clear that it's really a canonical definition. It might just be one text's definition and another would have a different way of placing it in its context. And you just go 'round and 'round and 'round in circles trying to, you know, clarify a situation which often isn't that clear in its essence. And that, to me, is hard. It's interesting, but it's hard. And it can be exhausting.

Later, he expresses particular satisfaction with the puzzle-solving and creative aspects of his work.

"Do I Think What I Do Is Important?" MIRI-U catalogers enjoy catalog work. However, they disagree on how much involvement they want with areas not obviously associated with cataloging. Margaret likes "just sitting there doing my thing," which includes interacting daily with subject librarians in her specialty. But "what I like most about what I do is being Sherlock Holmes every day." Describing one instance where her knowledge of Roman and non-Roman alphabets, previous interlibrary loan experience, and a liking for puzzle-solving led to identifying correct author and title information for a transliterated work, she declares, "That's the kind of thing that I enjoy most." Chris represents a different viewpoint. She finds excitement in new things, and spends a portion of her time in various subject libraries as part of a cataloging team:

> It was very nice for a couple of years to just catalog and work with colleagues who just did cataloging. But after that time I was really glad to have the opportunity to start breaking out a little bit again. . . . Cataloging here means pretty much sitting at your desk all day and cataloging. I felt I really missed that lack of contact with students and people coming into the library. . . . I have more of a context for cataloging now. I see the places and talk to the people who are using these materials.

Chris's blend of special projects and regular catalog work illustrates a level of personal responsibility and an expanded work world that are becoming more the norm for MIRI-U catalogers. As Elizabeth puts it, "In the old days, [it was] 'These books are always here and a truckload of them will be wheeled into your cubicle, and when you get them done they'll be wheeled out'". Now, says Chris, "What I do, initially, is talk with the [subject librarians] and find out what they need, if they have any special cataloging needs and if they have any special concerns about the materials—special features that need to be brought out."

Another example of blending is combining reference work with cataloging. One result of the rise of national bibliographic utilities has been a reduction in time spent cataloging and an increase in time spent offering direct assistance to the library's uses (Intner 1993). As a cataloger, Brooke finds that "I know the classification numbers and the cataloging—I know how to search NOTIS or MIRIUCAT better than most [reference] people." A serials cataloger knows serial titles and "can almost off the top . . . say to a patron, 'Yes, we've got it,' or 'No, we don't.'" Continues Brooke, "Our experience is very immediately and obviously transferable to reference. It helps [in being] a better reference person." However, some catalogers give negative value to expanding their tasks to include even cataloging-related user assistance work. For example, although catalogers in HSS are eligible to do information desk work, there is a pervasive feeling "that a professional catalog librarian probably shouldn't do that. . . . It [is] the idea of not putting pressure on people to have to feel like they want to do it" (Chris). Subject library catalogers exhibit the greatest blending of both tasks. Mike believes he spends 50 percent of his time doing original cataloging, 25 percent on reference, and 25 percent on committees and his own research interests. Essentially, he says, "if I'm not on reference, I start cataloging." And Elaine finds she varies cataloging with reference, editing, and other processing activities over the length of a day.

In commenting on the work of catalogers, one reference librarian observed that they must have a "legalistic" mind-set—one that is enamored with details and puzzle-solving. An online searcher believes that the "learning curve [of cataloging] is so high" (Pat). A subject bibliographer, Rose thinks that "cataloging would be very difficult [to do], as it is a whole body of complexity. [It] sounds staggering." Margaret reflects the sentiments of many MIRI-U catalogers when she says, "In the end, if every single comma and semicolon, and every single field is not exactly correct, somebody comes and complains because they can't do their job right because I didn't do mine. And they accuse catalogers of being such nitpickers!" Brooke suggests it is difficult to do cataloging on anything other than a regular basis because "it's too much detail driven." However, Brooke also noted her difficulty in creating only brief—rather than full— records: "It was very difficult for me to experience the process, [although] some access is better than no access."

As a set of tasks, catalog work is a continual decision-making process: As material arrives, it must be evaluated, described, and given a location in order to be useful. Even with a large body of rules, standards, and interpretation available to catalogers, "there's lots of undeveloped areas and weaknesses and odd inconsistencies" (Andy). At MIRI-U, basic goals for many catalogers include to "work like mad to try and get caught up" with incoming and backlogged materials and to "have excellent, excellent turnaround time." Margaret finds she varies between trying to be a perfectionist in support of the subject library for which she catalogs and "making choices on a case-by-case basis." Ultimately, her primary goal reflects that of most MIRI-U catalogers: "To do the best that I can and have some fun while I'm doing it."

Reference Work

During the eighteenth, nineteenth, and early twentieth centuries, university faculty and library directors believed faculty and students should (and could) find their own library materials and information. However, from the mid-1930s forward, librarian-staffed reference service areas developed in all types of academic libraries (Shiflett 1981). *Reference service* is now commonly defined as "personal assistance provided to users in the pursuit of information" (Bunge 1980, 468). Service connotes contributing to the welfare of others. But what is reference "work"? Bunge believes reference service comprises three kinds of work: (1) information *service*, which consists of finding needed information for the user or assisting the user in finding such information; (2) *instruction* in library use, consisting of helping users learn the skills they need to find and use library materials; and (3) *guidance*, in which users are assisted in choosing library materials appropriate to their educational, informational, or recreational needs (468–69; emphasis added).

Reference work engages both a librarian and a library user. Mary, a reference librarian, defines it as providing "service that has integrity and that offers either the right answer or the right method or methods for people to find what it is that they are looking for." MIRI-U librarians use active verbs when describing reference work: providing, explaining, assisting.

This work is both proactive and reactive: the former when tasks anticipate needs and advance services; the latter when in response to direct user statement of need. At MIRI-U, reference work is perceived as more variable than catalog or collection work. Librarians see it as encompassing a number of different tasks, done in a multitude of locations, during an array of times, in response to differing levels of need, by librarians from a range of units, and carried out to various degrees of completion and satisfaction.

As is similarly true in the area of collections, doing reference work and being a reference librarian can be two different things. A reference librarian is a member of a reference department or has reference work as a dominant, primary responsibility. If a librarian is not a member of such a designated unit but staffs a reference desk on some regular basis, she or he is considered as doing, more specifically, reference *desk* work. At MIRI-U, librarians whose primary tasks are with collection or catalog work may also do reference desk work. They do not call themselves reference librarians and consider it secondary work.

Librarians with primary reference work responsibilities describe themselves in terms such as "I am a reference librarian in the areas of . . . ." They then follow with phrases such as "bibliographic instruction . . . reference desk service . . . database searching." Typically, reference work includes the tasks of class instruction, database searching, collection work, and reference desk service. Although all reference librarians work at reference desks, in HSS's main reference service unit only some do database searching or reference collection development. Librarians in subject libraries are apt to do all four tasks and comment that "we do everything." Thus, even though reference librarians at MIRI-U do not have identical job descriptions, they work within the same broad set of tasks. Sandy represents most reference librarians:

> Well, my job description is Reference Librarian. I guess there is a little bit of outreach written in there somewhere. I would say I work on the reference desk, usually one shift a day (two or three hours). I'm involved in teaching, and that's on a sort of sporadic basis. It's terribly busy in the fall and there's almost none in the summer. . . . I've been given some of the responsibility for developing new classes. . . . I do searching—maybe not every day. I do a lot of informal user education at the desk. . . . I'm involved in doing things like professional organizations and librarywide things that don't really have to do with my absolute job at [this library]. But that's considered part of our job and so it's OK that I work on that during the day. Oh, and some things I'm sort of asked to do and some things I've sort of cooked up for myself.

Reference work is done at a reference desk, from an office, in any public area where a user queries a librarian, over the phone, via e-mail and the Internet, or through written correspondence. A basic characteristic of reference work is that when users need help, "they'll come and get one of us, whether we're on the desk or not" (Sandy); or as Galen puts it, when users need help, "we're all fair game—there's no hiding."

Reference desk-related activities dominate MIRI-U librarians' thinking about reference work for several reasons. First, this object and its immediate surroundings are central in librarians' definition of reference work because it is *the* place identified when a user wanting assistance says Where do I go for help? Second, it symbolizes how closely one is associated with being a reference librarian. Those who do reference-related tasks as secondary work do not link themselves to the desk, whereas, for example, Shelley, for whom such work is primary, describes herself as "a reference librarian, which means I work the reference desk." Nancy feels reference desk work is "the most important part" of her job as a reference librarian. Those with reference as their primary work place other tasks as secondary. The locus of much reference work is at or near "the desk." Every library facility has at least one reference desk. Units with no obvious place for reference service are physically arranged so that answering questions is carried out by anyone within reach of users.

Third, reference desk work is one of the very few tasks over which librarians have little control. Although they usually have some choice over when, how often, and how long they sit at a reference desk, the desk itself is staffed during set hours and days over the course of each academic year. Librarians must arrange their other tasks around it. MIRI-U reference librarians average fifteen hours each week at a reference desk, which significantly reduces the degree of control they feel over their remaining work.

The close connection between reference librarians and reference desks extends even to placement of their offices. Nancy likes having her office "around the corner" from the reference desk. Galen's is up a couple of floors in another part of the science library, and because "it's kind of hard being that far away," he has "made sort of an outpost in the reference desk area." Sandy adds, "I feel I am sort of isolated in my office," which is on the other side of a book stack area from her unit's reference desk.

The pace of activity at a MIRI-U reference desk varies by time of academic year, number of librarians staffing it, and whether questions are of a simple or complex nature. In one subject library, "if it's spring break, there's nobody in the library"; in another, librarians are handling the most complex questions of the year at that time. At reference desks generally, "in the middle of the term it peaks and things get really busy, and then you go to the end and people are taking finals and you don't see anyone until they come back" (Pat). Most desks are staffed from building opening until around eight p.m. Monday through Friday, some on Saturday and Sunday. Although many units staff with one librarian, others routinely use at least two. Due to the small number of staff in her subject library, Shelley notes that during summer vacations she actually has more desk hours than during academic terms.

Answering Questions. Some reference work literature groups questions into categories such as directional, informational, reference, and extended; some consider questions either very easy or very difficult (St. Clair and Aluri 1977; Childers, Lopata, and Stafford 1991; Alafiatayo, Yip, and Blunden-Ellis 1996). MIRI-U librarians divide questions into basic and advanced. Usually, basic reference work requires the use of MIRIUCAT, database terminals, and standard materials such as comprehensive encyclopedias, indexes, and general serials.

As the degree of complexity of questions and responses rises, librarians envision their work as moving from basic to advanced. Most MIRI-U librarians see the main HSS reference service unit as working with both levels of questions, but with emphasis clearly on the basic. Subject library librarians and bibliographers view their type of reference work as almost exclusively advanced. A subject bibliographer, Judith finds that:

> there will be phone calls from faculty and graduate students and undergraduate students that need to be followed up on. By the time they're calling me, it's very often not something I can answer in two minutes or off the top of my head. So some days I feel as if I'm on call for reference work all day long. . . . It's only a small part of my job description, [but] at certain times—[like] when students are writing papers, I can spend my whole day on reference questions.

Elizabeth, also a subject bibliographer, says that "since I know something about the disciplines, I also do specialized subject reference. And that's when reference [librarians] send someone to me. They can't handle the question at the desk and they want to fall back, or it's too broad, or students and teachers come directly to me because I've met them in class." Librarians in subject libraries stress they respond to both question levels, but with the weight on advanced. As a member of such a collection, Elaine points out that:

> the main difference, of course, is that no one is assigned a particular slot of time they have to be there to do reference. It's just [users] come in and whoever is available helps out the person. And I think that in some sense our [area] is harder to learn. You have to develop a more synergistic viewpoint. In a large reference department you can be more or less a specialist or you can call in specialists when someone needs really in-depth reference help. And here we have to keep in mind there's a whole field of things, from vertical file to publications to departmental collections to audiovisual material, that might be consulted in any given case for a person who is looking for a subject. So you're thinking in a broader range of materials.

Study of user psychology and mastery over resources are characteristics of reference work for, as Jesse Hauk Shera (1970, 47) observed, "reference librarians know what a chore it is, what a task it is, to discover what the patron really wants." MIRI-U librarians employ various techniques for finding out what is really wanted. For example, Sandy remembers what it can be like to be a user. Because as a student "I was somebody who never asked—never," she now takes a very direct approach with users, such as "wandering around those terminals asking everybody, 'Are you finding what you want?'" Fran believes she can also get more information from users by going beyond their original question and "asking two or three more questions, and they are just like, 'Well, what do you do this for?' [I say] 'I need to know more about what you are looking for so I can give you the right tools', or words to that effect." She adds, "I always try to get a context. . . . Try to give people another reason for using the materials, give them some scope, some additional information that will help them use the materials at a later date for something else—for related things." One of her goals is "trying to make the next time you deal with that same question better, filling in the blanks." But, cautions Mark, "Never say an absolute 'no' to anything," adding that "usually the original question sounds hopeless, but by the time you start to negotiate it and find out what the implications are . . . sometimes our understanding moves, sometimes what they are looking for can move slightly—timewise or geographically or something, [and yet we can] still accommodate the same subject."

Negotiating is a constant in reference work. Galen provides an example when he talks about trying to minimize waiting time for users lined up at a desk:

> You pretty much have to take them one after the other. And you don't know that one person might take you two seconds to answer, the next one may take ten minutes. And you really can't sort them out. I tried juggling them, you know, What's your question? What's *your* question? And then that leads to all kinds of hard feelings. And you think you can do the simple one first and then you'll have time to do the hard one, but that gets very messy.

At desks, insufficient time associated with assisting one user after another has an especially high negative value. In commenting on a previous desk schedule, Nancy notes that "two [two-hour] shifts virtually every day was exhausting work. . . . Even if questions were not very demanding of me, it was very tiring to be there and to be constantly [answering] one question right after the other. And when you got off the desk, with that type of environment . . . I'd be tired for a half hour. And not be as productive."

As for the tools of reference work, MIRI-U librarians first use those in their immediate work vicinity regardless of format, then those that support the needs of the query regardless of location. However, Mary reflects, different reference units emphasize certain kinds of resources. Her unit tends more toward computer-based than print tools. She gives an example:

> When I [first] came here, if somebody had come up and
> said, "I want the *Reader's Guide*," you'd take him to the
> *Reader's Guide*. If somebody comes up and says [that now],
> well, we have it online, we have it in print in two locations,
> and we have it or something similar on CD-ROM files.

Indeed, feeling more competent with online than print-based tools,
another librarian in the same department is currently concentrating on
studying print resources related to her subject areas. And James expresses
concern "that reference librarians in particular have to spend increased
amounts of time with each person explaining the technology as well as
how the library is structured." Bob agrees, commenting that "most of our
time now is interpreting new equipment to individuals coming in, so we
can help them to help themselves to the material that they want. That's
kind of what I view reference as right now: to help people to help themselves do this. Because it's an experiential occupation, really. Anybody
doing any research has [ultimately] to do it themselves."

Among the newer tasks in reference work is development of online
resources that serve two generally separate goals. One is user self-suffi-
ciency, which is highly valued by those doing reference work. A Knowledge Navigator fits this goal. A dedicated terminal contains information
on both how to find and how to do things. For example, a user can learn
how to use MIRIUCAT. And under *R* of the alphabetical menu, entries
include "rare books, recalls, reference, renewals, reserve readings, restroom,
the RLIN bibliographic file," etc. Librarians developing this resource are
continually adding files to it: "More quick reference stuff—the 'how do I
find . . . ?' related to various subjects" (Susan).

The second goal for electronic tools is to have online indices that
"kind of pool all of our knowledge in an organized way" (Galen). Reference librarians create these latter tools primarily for their own use—for
"hard questions I've found the answer to," especially those "we've dug
and uncovered in an unlikely place" (Galen). For example, says Patti,
"[when] we spend a half hour finding the answer to some difficult reference questions, rather than just try to put it in memory, we now put it in
a computer database at the reference desk."

The continuous appearance of new tools, especially electronic ones,
prompts Brenda to comment about hearing "a lot of talk about burnout"

among those doing reference work. In considering an electronic future, she asks, "How are we going to handle the walk-in traffic and then still sit at a computer and answer Internet questions? I don't know; it'll be interesting."

Satisfaction. Reference work is not for everyone. Elizabeth illustrates this when she says, "I don't enjoy anymore the kind of interaction with students you get at the reference desk, where it's this question and that question and some other question. I enjoy more the assembling of a body of information applied to a question that a student has." Yet Mark and Galen are attracted to reference work "because it's so unpredictable" and "totally uncontrolled." Those who enjoy reference work respond positively to such challenges. Nancy, who finds it "intriguing to get mind puzzles," believes that reference is a "perfect match" for her interests, personal and professional needs and goals. Elaine illustrates the combination of liking public contact and being challenged. She notes that in her archives, "we get a whole lot of the same kinds of questions as any reference department does, but the fun comes in when you get something that you've never been asked before and you have to start exploring a whole new line of thinking. And then when you come up with something for [that user], too."

Dissatisfaction is generally expressed in terms of loss of autonomy and lack of completion. Jan is frustrated that "the work on [a particular project] gets done in bits and pieces: pickup time. Two minutes here, and two there. In reference work, the thing is you can't schedule large blocks of time." Mary speaks to a lack of completion that is felt acutely by several reference librarians:

> I'm not indifferent to the outcome. When somebody leaves the desk and we've worked on something together, or I've worked hard to do something for them and never see them again—. Over the years I've found that I'm not very satisfied with feeling so disengaged from the outcome or the output.

Yet, most reference librarians truly enjoy this kind of work and would agree with Nancy that "the interactions that we have with people are the most important things we do. . . . [E]very interaction over the reference desk or every interaction that I have [is] another chance to make an impact of some sort."

Learning–Teaching–Training Work

MIRI-U librarians may not recognize this as a category. It is not the primary work of any single librarian; yet it warrants more than secondary status. Regardless of their dominant work, librarians give significant time and concern to these tasks.

Although librarians use the terms interchangeably in conversation, there are differences in their meanings. Librarians use *teaching* when talking about students becoming self-sufficient in libraries. It is strongly associated with course-related library instruction. They use *training* to describe instruction in a specific skill. It generally refers to sessions for library personnel and to on-the-spot activities in front of computer terminals for anyone. *Learning* has several associations. There is learning as a fundamental part of being an academic librarian, learning for self-enhancement, and learning in order to do teaching and training.

Whatever its meaning, learning is an active process, a "coming to know," and a fundamental aspect of thinkwork (Zuboff 1988). It is highly valued by academic librarians. Sandy represents the views of many when she comments that "I like being with people [who] are interested in learning all the time. I'm happy I ended up in a profession where I'm expected to continue learning, and sort of forced—. Yeah, I'm forced to, and that's fine with me. I love it. And to be surrounded by other people that are like that . . . !" The more pragmatic Bob believes "if you've had library training, you've got the basics and most of the things you need. And whatever thing you go into, you're able to do it." Indeed, all it takes for Bob to learn to do something new is to be told he probably cannot do it.

MIRI-U librarians appear to be among those professionals who are determined to engage in lifelong learning (see Ruiz Quintanilla and Wilpert 1988). In commenting on what she would do if she retired from the library, Patti says, "For a day-to-day sort of thing, take classes. I mean, I'm not ready for the elder hostels yet, but they have great programs. . . . I want to be a lifelong learner." Chris values the current diversity of her work because it gives her the opportunity for "learning how to train people, learning how to develop procedural things, learning about hiring." And after twelve years as a cataloger, Margaret finds she still simply enjoys "learning different things and not doing exactly the same thing every day."

For these and other librarians, learning is part and parcel of one's work. It may be seen as "coming with the job," as Sandy illustrates above. Or it can be an unexpected part of work, as when Brenda finds that being a reference librarian is "more interesting than I anticipated. . . . It's actually very interesting and I've learned a lot." Many librarians also consciously choose to learn more by keeping up with what is going on in a particular field in academic librarianship or in a subject field. They frequently express interest in areas outside their regular responsibilities.

Librarians believe learning is part of being responsible in the conduct of their work. This leads to the notion of learning for self-enhancement. MIRI-U librarians take pride in improving on and mastering tasks, and on gaining knowledge for its own sake. They set no time, location, or type of task limit on learning. Tony illustrates this when he says, "I've learned a lot from being on [a reorganization] task force . . . that I bring into other meetings. And I can see right away how far ahead I am in what I've learned [about] trying to get people to focus on issues." Sandy reflects on a process she developed for learning everything she could about print materials in her collection: "My God, it was so tedious. It took forever to do that. But then by the end, [I] was so good. . . . I feel like now with the databases it's the same thing. It takes longer, but the more databases I know how to use, [the more] I know just what to do." A reference librarian, Patti comments on the positive value of having catalogers work at a reference desk:

> Because they had all the background knowledge of the online catalog and they knew the collection so well, I learned so much from them. And I know all of [us] did, because we learned much more about the catalog and other stuff—just how we handle the books and the journals. And then it was good to see them realize what we did out there.

In reflecting on previous learning, Galen values having "the broader picture. When we were doing some of the training and stuff like that, it happens that our OPAC has a lot of features, and I found it very useful having been [an online] searcher because I'd spent a lot of hours planning searches for people and using the system and learning its ins and outs and that sort of thing. That was very helpful—not in a deep programming sense but in a how-to-use-it sense."

Librarians believe learning is valuable as well as fun, and they try to get others to see that as well. Thus, they believe in learning in order to transmit knowledge to library users and staff members. In separate comments, Brenda, Sandy, and Fran convey this in talking about learning and databases:

> Brenda: We're constantly getting new databases; we're learning about the Internet; new technology. . . . Things are changing so rapidly that sometimes we're in the office saying, "Oh, I just can't learn another database." Oh, you know, a hundred different details. And to be expected to know that.

> Interviewer: So how do you learn it all?

> Brenda: You just have to figure it out—flying by the seat of your pants. There isn't any other way to be able to then explain it to the patrons.

> Sandy: I try to make myself sit down and try some questions before it's me and the patron sitting down and doing it. I mean, that's sort of embarrassing.

> Brenda: [Stopping is] more based on necessity rather than a [personal] decision of when to stop learning. I think we try to learn as much as we can, and we sort of gauge what we need to know based on the kind of questions that we get.

> Fran: We need to make our staff familiar enough with [databases] so that they know when it might be appropriate to suggest [a specific resource] to a user. . . . I learn by reading, discussion, things coming over the terminal, reading both in library-related things and newspapers, and training [sessions].

Because librarians highly value learning, they see its never-ending nature as distinctly positive.

Librarians' use of the concept of teaching has a number of antecedents. The most prominent is that librarians see aspects of the library they believe users do not either find to be self-explanatory or realize the value of. Teaching, then, enhances understanding. An example of this perspective is Peg's comment that as a specialist in a particular subject library, "it's my responsibility to teach what I can about it, to encourage the use of it, to make it known." Whether a librarian's goal is to explain the Internet, CD-ROMs, or how archival documents relate to each other, this view focuses on "teaching [users] how to find the information that they want" (Shelley).

A related goal is to enhance a user's proficiency in working with the library's resources and services. Michele, a data librarian, noted that although "they train you to work with the written word, people have not had that kind of training in numbers, [so I] teach them what kinds of questions to ask of numbers, what kinds of red flags to watch for." Or, as Sandy says, "[It's] helping people to learn how to help themselves." At MIRI-U, teaching is valued—not as highly in many minds as conducting research, but it is valued. Librarians acknowledge that positive value and see teaching as having a place in their work lives. Increasing understanding and proficiency of students, faculty, and essentially anyone on campus is why "we are a part [of the university. Why] it's so terribly important for us to be an active part of the university's teaching and research mission" (Peg).

When speaking of teaching, most librarians envision a setting where they are the single instructor in a classroom or library location with a group of students. They always use the term when referring to being an instructor-of-record in a university course. Some also use it when discussing one-on-one work with users in the library. Regardless of setting, librarians believe that "what you present to [students] is going to influence what sort of information they are going to find and how they're going to find it and how they're going to work with it" (Judith).

Michele envisions her work as having only two components: One is to "get data out to the people who need it. . . . The other is to help people or to teach people how to use data intelligently and correctly." She uses an example to illustrate why she believes teaching is important work:

When I do a class, I'm not going in and saying, "Well, here's this data set and here's the numbers, and this is how you do it." I'm saying, "Look at what the real numbers are. It doesn't make it less of a problem, but put some perspective in it. . . . Ask questions about the numbers. . . . [Learn] to say, when someone puts something up in percentages and there are no numbers or you don't know what the size of a population was or what the size of the sample was, 'Well, that's magnificent, but I can have 100 percent increase in something, but if I originally had one person that's not exactly the major drop in the bucket'. . . . It's how you report something. Go back and check where the numbers came from." [I] teach them what kinds of questions to ask.

As curator in a subject library, Peg also believes that "teaching is an important part of what I do, [whether it is] a seminar on editing historical documents [or] special courses in honors." She finds it odd to think about separating librarianship from teaching. Even the topic of retirement includes the comment that "I probably would continue to do some teaching, either at the university or elsewhere."

The most common kind of teaching is bibliographic instruction (BI). Librarians with specific instruction responsibilities, and others with general reference, subject bibliography, or subject library responsibilities do this work. They speak of BI classes in terms of "lower division" and "upper division." Librarians teach freshman and sophomore classes the "facilitating skills" necessary for working with basic resources and services. Junior, senior, and graduate classes receive instruction on resources related to the narrower focus of advanced academic courses. Librarians in HSS also use the terms to distinguish between general reference area librarians and subject bibliographers. The former work with introductory courses, whereas the latter focus on advanced courses in the departments of their specific disciplinary areas. In other facilities and in subject libraries, librarians with an array of public area responsibilities do BI across the range of academic course levels.

As is traditional in BI, librarians gear content to class assignments (Farber 1995). Typically, a librarian responds to a course instructor's request for BI. She then elicits information on class focus, topics, assignments, structure, and level of student knowledge. She assesses the topics, identifying and reviewing relevant resources and services, deciding on the degrees of complexity associated with resources and class level, and drafts a session. She prepares the resources and materials to be viewed, used, or given out. And she hopes all equipment pieces will be present and will work. Illustrating the complexity of BI work, Nancy describes an upcoming session where the topics "are incredibly difficult. [I] will take the students into government documents, interviewing of ethnic groups, treaty rights, etc." Her strategies include having students do online as well as manual searches of indexes and explaining interlibrary loan as "we will not have all the sources" relevant to their topics.

Connecting BI content to course-specific topics and assignments can serve as a constraint to reusing session materials. The high probability of change in instructors, topics, assignments, and relevant resources means librarians regularly rework lecture notes, examples, handouts, and instructional strategies. The other major constraint for this kind of activity is limited time. Most BI sessions are one-time events, and often an endless variety of resources relevant to the topics must somehow, says Mary, fit into "fifty minutes or two hours at the most. So even if people tell you that they'd rather see a video and have six hours of hands-on and have things more integrated, you don't get to do it." Fundamentally, Fran concludes, BI means "we're bringing the students into the room and showing them where tools are, discussing the use of particular tools, and occasionally getting enough time to work with the class so that we can sit them down in another room and do some demonstrations."

Regardless of the complexity of the task, librarians conduct BI sessions because they are convinced such information aids students—from those who will do fine on their own to those "who will make a point of avoiding the library because it seems utterly inaccessible." Mary, a general reference librarian, illustrates her comment on student bewilderment by role-playing one who "comes up and starts the question by saying, 'I never use the library. I don't know what I'm doing.' But it's like, 'My hand is forced. Here I am! I have to ask you a question. . . . I've been here for six hours and I haven't found anything. I'm finally turning myself in. Can you help me? I'm about ready to go crazy.'" Various librarians relate that even new graduate students can feel "overwhelmed" by the library. Several take the topic of anxiety directly into their BI lectures. Mary takes an institutional tack:

> One of the things that I try to mention is, "The library, to some degree, is your tuition dollars at work. This is yours as much as the student union or classroom facilities. This is yours. And it's a magnificent collection and one that you should be proud of as part of this institution that you belong to." They need to develop a sense of the place as something that they own, or can own, intellectually or just in terms of a specific item.

Fran, a subject librarian, seeks to connect with students on a personal level:

> I always say, "If I had only three minutes with you, I would say: Ask questions. We encourage you to browse, we encourage you to look around and see what's here or to look at our materials, to see the guides we have. But please don't fail to ask. Don't walk away thinking we don't have something."

Such perspectives are based on the belief that, as Mary puts it, "some students really need some encouragement to enter in" to the intellectual activity.

In general, these MIRI-U librarians acknowledge that BI is an incomplete assist to students and look upon it as progressive work. They feel students respond best when the latter participate in sessions from lower- through upper-division courses, then "[we find] the seniors actually do very well: They write good papers, they do use library resources" (Judith).

The librarians have mixed views of how BI will fit into their work at MIRI-U in the future. Some see the advent of the electronic library as reducing the need for the lower-division, introductory sessions. With protocols for CD-ROMS and various other online tools moving toward standardization, they believe there may be less need for librarians to spend time explaining such resources to students. And knowledge navigators for

N.C. CENTRAL UNIVERSITY
SCHOOL OF LIBRARY & INFO. SCI.

specific resources will provide self-teaching modules. However, other librarians are experiencing an increase in requests from upper-division instructors and graduate students. They see this as the trend. It is likely that both groups of librarians are seeing the same future. At some point, electronic resources will be like books: Generally, everyone is familiar with how they work. However, that time has not arrived at MIRI-U so it is likely that as students and instructors experience some number of sessions during undergraduate years, they will expect bibliographic instruction in its narrower and deeper form to be present for them as they advance through the university.

Not all MIRI-U librarians like BI work. These librarians fall into two groups: Those who do not like the context and those who do not like the content. The former believe there is a distinct personality suitable for BI work that they do not have. It seems that context-negative librarians basically are uncomfortable working with anonymous groups. Such librarians feel ill at ease with the classroom-type setting. They develop and do BI work because it is a responsibility, but they get their enjoyment from working with students on a one-on-one basis. On the other hand, content-negative librarians do not mind groups. What makes them shudder is reflected in Pat's comment: "[It is the] stuff you teach in a library class. It's teaching 'This is a book, this is an index, this is the online catalog.' Blah." Content-negative BI librarians do not like to dwell on basics. They see excitement for both students and themselves in working with topics and problems associated with advanced-level BI or subject-specific training sessions. In fact, both content- and context-negative BI librarians hit their stride when engaged in training.

This generally in-house activity occurs in order to fill a specific knowledge gap. Librarians consider training part of supervising when providing it to subordinates. They view it as collegial when providing it to peers. And they treat it as egalitarian when training the two groups together. Librarians view their own training as continuing education. They give and attend workshops and programs because of a felt need to gain competency over those things they see as related to their work. Elizabeth notes, for example, that "I'm feeling incompetent in electronic sources because I don't have time to play around and master them. But I'm looking forward to some workshops and things that will give me an edge on that."

This work has a range of dimensions: It may be a one-time workshop or a program comprising several sessions. There is a defined need, a specified topic, and the structure frequently includes a hands-on component. It is home-grown and carried out in the library or on campus. MIRI-U librarians have developed in-house training that is the height of collegiality—offering, asking, and depending on each other for keeping current in many aspects of their work.

Training runs the gamut from informal "demos" through bag lunches to formal classes with exercises and scripts for presenters. Demos and bag lunches tend to be spur-of-the-moment activities. Bag lunches are occasions for "somebody to show you things," and the individual librarian decides what "thing" is worth hearing about. More frequent is the demo—an informally structured demonstration session commonly related to learning or updating knowledge about a resource.

At MIRI-U, purchase of a new electronic tool is the most frequent occasion for a demo. The ever-increasing number of CD-ROMS and databases makes continual training and being trained regular parts of one's work. Some items are structured similarly to already known tools, and training is then of the demo variety. Other resources have unique or inadequately described structures and requirements. Before librarians will put the latter out for user consumption, they master it themselves. Patti says, "[When a new product arrives] generally I have a demo. . . . I just give [staff] the basics. I can't give them tests or force them to sit down there, take the time to learn it. [But] if they don't take the time to learn it on their own, they have trouble explaining it to patrons." In her unit, adds Fran, "we try to have a structured session with the rest of the reference staff on tools that we're sure people will be starting to use. . . . We need to make our staff familiar enough with them so that they know when it might be appropriate to suggest it to a user." The electronic aspects of work, in particular, mean a steep growth curve. As the curve goes up, so does the frequency of training sessions—as Sandy puts it, "every two months there are more terminals in reference with more databases up, and more things to learn."

Librarians make training more formal when a complex new product or service is being unveiled and a large number of library staff will be responsible for its use. Because of their collegial nature, such programs also provide BI context-negative librarians with great amounts of pleasure and satisfaction. Galen demonstrates both of these findings in commenting on a typical situation where formal training is used:

> I was involved from the beginning in implementing and so forth our local OPAC. I was involved in the staff training, but I did enjoy that. . . . They were all colleagues and that kind of environment, and that was very satisfying. . . . We had [a couple of hundred] staff that all had to be trained on this new system. So we had to set up a system of classes and exercises and so forth. I was on one of the committees, and it fell to me to write the script that other people were going to use in these training sessions. I'd never done anything quite like that. It was really gratifying to write that and then to sit in on one of them and to watch somebody read your script.

As indicated earlier, MIRI-U librarians learn from and also train each other. They exhibit a shared commitment to knowledge that Susan Albers Mohrman and Susan G. Cohen (1995) attribute to being in a lateral organization: one where an understanding of ideas and frameworks of thinking cuts across units and departments. Learning, teaching, and training are a Mobius strip for these librarians. Continuous learning is both a personal characteristic of many librarians and, essentially, a job requirement. Teaching and training are fundamental parts of the library's support of the university's mission. To be able to train each other in order to then teach library users, librarians must learn continuously.

Primary Work and Behavior
In talking about how people create their own realities, Lee Ross and Richard E. Nisbett (1991, 154) point out that studies of physicians, clerics, entrepreneurs, and even rock stars show they all began by making choices that "reflected their personal preferences and capacities. Their choices, in turn, placed them in social contexts that allowed, even compelled, them to further develop and display those preferences and capacities." It appears that MIRI-U librarians follow this same track.

For every librarian, certain tasks are chosen and become favored over others—ultimately combining to reflect a cluster of tasks and activities upon which librarians spend the greatest amount of time or by which they define themselves. The tasks making up this primary (or dominant) work give librarians an anchor—a work-associated identity that contributes to a definition of self. Primary work also illuminates a set of shared meanings in that librarians doing similar work believe they understand what each other does. This leads them to compare themselves to those doing different work and to make distinctions between their own work and that of other librarians. Using the concept of primary work, MIRI-U librarians make connections internally within their own working group and externally to other groups of librarians. Primary work provides individual librarians with a grounded psychological orientation and identity (Hackman and Oldham 1980; Braude 1983).

In this chapter, we have seen that MIRI-U librarians are very involved in four types of work: collection, catalog, reference, and learning-teaching-training. Collection work deals with building, molding, and preserving the library's holdings. Many of the tasks and time involvements that define this category are not visible to library users. However, both they and librarians use the results to define MIRI-U library's basic reputation and standing, on and off campus.

Catalog work is information control work. Librarians take a raw item containing myriad information and give it an identity. Through descriptive, subject, and authority tasks, they not only determine its location in the intellectual world (next to other materials on the same topic) but also influence how users will think of it and what things users will relate to it. Reference work gives MIRI-U's library a human face and personality. The librarians' emphasis is placed not on the library's materials but, rather, on the nature of its relationship with users. Tasks revolve around identifying and clarifying users' needs so that users (and librarians) are satisfied with the support the library offers. Finally, learning-teaching-training work focuses on knowledge. These tasks enable librarians to do their work. Whether in support of users or for their own understanding of tasks, MIRI-U librarians continuously engage in this triad.

The beliefs and behaviors of MIRI-U librarians regarding their primary work illustrate basic findings of a number of studies of different professions and jobs; that is, work orientation and involvement, and work ethic values, are related directly to work behavior and performance (see

Roberson 1990). Development of beliefs about the nature and importance of what they do influences MIRI-U librarians to behave accordingly. Their work forms a central, though not exclusive, life interest for them. This theme of primary work centrality runs throughout their description of tasks and job activities. Work orientation for the majority of librarians is intrinsic; that is, the actual content and substance of their work is valued more than the salary, status, or other rewards it might bring. Their involvement with work suggests that it is a major component of their self-image. MIRI-U librarians identify themselves with and through their work, thus defining themselves in terms of those work roles (Braude 1983; Rabinowitz and Hall in Roberson 1990). Their equally strong work ethic values come through in beliefs about their library system and university.

NOTES

1. Beginning with this chapter, the MIRI-U librarians are extensively quoted, using pseudonyms. See the appendix for background on the librarians.

2. A variant of Albert Kenneth Rice's (1963) notion of a hierarchy of tasks within organizations.

3. Academic librarians use *patrons* and *users* as general terms, and *faculty*, *undergraduates* and *graduates* when classing people by role. *User* reflects an assumption that all these groups expect to *use something* connected with a library, be that a source, a service, or a librarian.

3. The University and the Library

In critiquing relationships between employees and their organizations, Denise M. Rousseau and Kimberly A. Wade-Benzoni (1995) usefully divide the recent Western past into three historical phases: emergent, bureaucratic, and adhocratic. The emergent phase is associated with the late eighteenth-century shift from cottage craftwork to centralized workplaces where managerial control was dominant and employee commitment to their work and place of work was based on there being fewer and fewer viable economic alternatives. The bureaucratic phase is defined by complex organizational hierarchies exemplified by administrative control over employees and development of long-term contractual relationships that stress employee socialization to organizational norms and the rise of job specialization. In this second phase, Rousseau and Wade-Benzoni define employee commitment as affective and of being one of continuance: Employees who "invest" in the organization fill the role of "company men" and climb career ladders within that organization or a small number of related organizations. "Careers were secure and stable, shaped by the organization, and directed toward movement up the hierarchy" (Howard 1995b, 10). The adhocratic phase is seen as the current model and represents a fundamental shift in the nature of work. Here, emphasis is on continuous skill development, less upward and more lateral career mobility, hiring flexibility that includes employees with only project or temporary contracts, and reorganization to flatten layers of existing hierarchy. There is an increase in self-supervising employees with managers serving as team facilitators or doing minimal integration of the work carried out by individuals. In this postindustrial phase, employee commitment is based on a sense of self: Those who feel "core" to the organization behave both as independent decision makers and as owners of the enterprise. Employees who have only temporary or project arrangements may feel a strong sense of connection with their work, but a more remote association with the organization's values and goals. Work becomes increasingly decentralized as a result of electronic technologies, and the sense of being an independent worker can include having one's workplace be at home or at a central organizational location. Rousseau and Wade-Benzoni envision the adhocratic phase as the likely future employment model.

This last model, however, is easily seen in universities and it is not new. Writers as divergent as John D. Millett (1962), Frederick Rudolph (1962), Dean E. McHenry (1977), and Burton J. Bledstein (1978) describe the typical faculty member at the beginning of the twentieth century as being not an employee, but a powerful and independent expert involved in institution-wide decision-making. Indeed, in 1986, Michael D. Cohen and James G. March coined the term "organized anarchies" to describe institutions of higher education in general. In 1977, J. Victor Baldridge et al. presented what they saw as common collegial organizational characteristics that seemed unique, however, when compared to the characteristics of industry, business, and government. Two particularly significant attributes are management by consensus and assumption that the leader's role is to be "first among equals" and a developer of professionals. It is within this framework of an independent, participating, "thinkworker" organizational culture that academic librarians go about their work.

MIRI-U

Like most public, research-dominated universities, MIRI-U is large and both physically and administratively decentralized. The main campus with its old traditional quad and several smaller, newer building clusters epitomize the university. Each area, such as the medical buildings with their "health sciences complex" feel, has its own ambience. Buildings are of varying ages, dating from MIRI-U's founding to the present.

People are polite in a way that one librarian calls "welcoming and distancing simultaneously," lest politeness be confused with approval. The impression is that warmth is shared among colleagues; caution or neutrality is shared with others. For librarians, MIRI-U is both a university and an institution. They associate "university" with students and faculty and "institution" with size and stress.

The University

> We are not a college—we are land grant and that means we have a lot of responsibilities that maybe a private, graduate-level research institution doesn't have. But it is the research aspects of the university that make it unique—that make it a valuable place to get an undergraduate education. Because you've got that option to access that more intense research type of mentality: the adventurer, the explorer. . . . An undergraduate education gets people thinking, but it's also there to build a framework of ideas and of knowledge, and of learning how to learn and how to process information. It gives you a basis [upon which] to expand and to think and to explore. (Michele)

MIRI-U librarians associate undergraduates with general reference areas in the humanities/social science and the science library buildings. Graduates, however, are the most frequent and heaviest users, and concentrate in the medical, science, and subject libraries. Some faculty use certain subject libraries and parts of MIRI-U's general libraries extensively; others "are never seen in the library" (Galen) by virtue of their field's orientation or their own lack of interest in library materials or services.

Undergraduate users range from "one achieving undergraduate who wanted to do research at the Library of Congress on Vietnam documents" (Nancy) to, more common, "those with a requirement that has to be met and no particular passion for meeting [it]" (Mark). Undergraduates and graduates also divide by discipline. Galen notes, for example, that:

> undergrads in most of the sciences and engineering and law aren't library users by and large. It's just not part of the curriculum. . . . They don't write the papers and have the kind of assignments that people in the social sciences do.

They've got their textbook, they've got their labs, they're very bound to that kind of environment. In fact, it's painfully obvious when they get to be seniors and finally have to write a paper for some senior engineering course that they have no idea how to proceed.

Graduate students "make up a large part of the desk activity" (Galen) in most subject libraries and across the library system in general. They interact with librarians as users and also as TAs and "gofers" for faculty members. Graduate students work with librarians more extensively than do undergraduates because the former are "in to do their long-term work" (Nancy) of a research paper, thesis, or dissertation. MIRI-U librarians look very positively on graduate students for a number of reasons. First and foremost, these users want to learn. More specifically, they "are learning to become researchers, become scholars" (Peg). They "are pretty directed. And they know the literature. And they know the 'language' [of their field] and, [although] they may have no clue what's out there to find," graduate students are often quite willing to ask for help (Sandy). They are especially intrigued by electronic resources, but "don't feel confident a lot of the time with doing [searching], and they need a lot of help" (Brenda). Second, librarians doing bibliographic instruction see graduate students as TAs. In that role, the students are learning how to be faculty, and librarians value the opportunity to connect with them during that evolution.

Where MIRI-U librarians see undergraduate use of libraries as assignment based and graduate use as training in doing research, they see faculty use as deeply focused on very narrow research efforts. This view corroborates similar findings about faculty in general (Blackburn and Lawrence 1995), faculty in specific fields (see, for example, Finkelstein 1984), and faculty in research universities (Clark 1987). As Lynne says, "the faculty are just doing such terribly interesting things. And things on a level that you just don't see in other places; that's really advanced." Librarians see faculty members as "too busy" to use the library unless it is absolutely necessary and sending a graduate student will not resolve their particular need. Thus, many librarians push access to tools such as MIRIUCAT into faculty offices, seeing it as an example of things they can do to assist faculty research and teaching efforts.

Subject bibliographers and subject librarians interact most frequently with faculty members. The library's holdings are the central topic bringing them together. "Librarians have always controlled book selection here; [faculty] suggest or make recommendations and we decide. And they accept this. They think this is appropriate" (Elizabeth). Librarians assert that neither they nor faculty like their time wasted and so office visits are only occasional. Karen lists routine contacts: meetings at common mailboxes, working with her library's faculty advisory committee, and attending faculty meetings and colloquia. She stresses that "what I do *for* my . . . faculty is important," including periodically surveying them to solicit information on research and teaching needs, and to gain ideas about her subject library. Librarians with advanced degrees or course work in the same subject field as their primary work have especially cordial relations with faculty. As Judith puts it, "They taught me a lot about the questions I should be asking them and the things that I should be thinking about." She is comfortable, for example, "writ[ing] them a long letter saying, 'I really do think you need to work library instruction into classes at earlier levels . . .' because I have proven myself in [their field]."

Relations with faculty distress many librarians at two points. First, librarians expect all users to abide by library policy, and find it irritating and unfair when exceptions are made for faculty offenders. Second, they believe faculty are more distant from "the cutting edge of change in libraries" (Mary) than they ought to be. Librarians conducting bibliographic instruction—who regularly see TAs as more current with technology and resources—are especially concerned. So are subject bibliographers, who believe most faculty are no longer aware of the extent of interdisciplinary materials existing across their research and teaching fields.

The Institution

MIRI-U enrolls close to 40,000 students and has a faculty and staff of close to 10,000; it is multicampus. Peg feels "there's a certain amount of loss of confidence in the whole educational experience here, and maybe at any large institution." "If," say quite a number of MIRI-U librarians, "[the university] could just be a little smaller." "So many of our problems are just sheer problems of numbers. You know, so many students chasing so few copies needing so much instruction and so many sections. It's just overly large" (Judith). There is a sense also that MIRI-U's physical size and arrangement decrease accessibility of librarians to each other and to colleagues across campus. Mary finds that "it's hard to break out of the unit and make connections with other people on campus. . . . It's such a huge campus, very distributed."

But there is a positive side to size, says Elizabeth. She believes that "people who work at smaller schools grow rather tired of or complacent with their faculty, [whereas] I have the constant stimulation of new people, . . . of new patrons coming in to use the collections." Brenda suggests that "you're more in tune with what's going on in the larger field, I think, at least more so than in a smaller school. . . . There's more going on, there's more action." To a degree, size contributes to MIRI-U's reputation as a research university with a large research library. As David notes, "[MIRI-U] just does everything big. We had to go after [a specific] grant, otherwise we'd have smaller numbers of equipment with smaller screens. With so many people [always visiting], we couldn't do otherwise. . . . We're setting out to be the lead library [in the Association of Research Libraries] on this project."

However, according to Lynne and a number of others, being big also equates to more bureaucracy:

> There is the absolutely endless bureaucracy at a place like [this]. It's just absolutely incredible. I continue to be staggered by how bureaucracy just gobbles you up. . . . The endless, endless, endless committees and task forces and everything that it takes to get anything at all accomplished. . . . You not only have to go up and down, but you have to go sideways too. . . . It isn't really so much that there's anybody who doesn't want you to accomplish something, it's just that you have to go 'round and 'round and 'round and 'round to end up getting it accomplished.

Even more to the point, she says, "one is never certain that the process that's being used is the most useful." Because Lynne is a unit head, she might be considered particularly aware of bureaucratic size and effect. Elizabeth has no current administrative connection, yet she also feels that "in a smaller place, if you have an idea you can carry it off without having to consult so many people. Here, if we want to make the most simple change in any procedure, you just spend hours and hours, sometimes weeks and sometimes months, having to consult everyone. And it's very frustrating." She muses that "in some ways, . . . the bureaucracy itself needs so much nurturing."

Regardless of annual levels of financial and facility support actually rendered by MIRI-U, librarians overall feel "we aren't getting new staff very readily any more" within the library and that there has been a "constant sort of erosion, quiet erosion [over time]" (Nancy, Judith). Most frequently, they mention loss of full-time librarian and support staff positions due to various institutional budgetary retrenchments and difficulties in filling vacated positions on a permanent basis. As the library internally reallocates and offers professional development and in-service training opportunities in lieu of salary increases, librarians see reference service hours cut, buildings closing earlier in the evenings, and library-paid subscriptions to their own professional literature become a thing of the past. And at the same time the legislature approves planning money for an archive building and discussion continues about an electronic text location in the Humanities & Social Sciences (HSS) library, librarians in another building hope to get air-conditioning "within the next five or six years—and we will then get maybe enough wiring so that we can support the electronic environment that [we already have] here" (Bob).

Over the past few years, librarians estimate that more than two dozen positions have been vacated with several lines lost to retrenchments. Almost every unit in MIRI-U's library system has been reduced by one to three people. Librarians believe that positions now get filled only when a vacancy occurs in a "single-person unit, and it [is] either hire someone or close the unit" (Fran). In some instances, librarians are hired on temporary funds, only to be lost to new budget reductions. As the sole person in her center, Michele illustrates what work life is like in small units:

> There is nobody to pass off the database stuff and the record-keeping to—all those little things that make libraries work, like making sure you have records of what you have, that are in an accessible format. It's like you get time to set up the

> system, but you never get time to enter the data. [I] don't
> have the support to do the job right. . . . [Ultimately,] I don't
> have enough time to sit back and look at what we're doing
> and look at the whole idea of making data and text available
> electronically. . . . The lack of financial support constrains
> you to the point that the only thing you have time for is to
> react.

Some units have lost up to half their student support. Elaine received
an increase in her student staff when an especially significant archive was
acquired from the university. Now, she finds, "on the whole, we're beginning to get some things done. It's going to be a shock when we go back to
life as usual—life with less."

MIRI-U librarians connect feelings of stress with insufficient support. Lynne, a unit head, speaks for many librarians when she says:

> I never feel as though I've really done anything because there
> are so many things waiting—that have been set aside for other
> things. . . . When I finish something, I'm just farther behind
> than when I started.

That pressure exists because:

> I'm doing all the clerical stuff that somebody else used to do
> for me. . . . I address all my own letters, I do photocopying.
> . . . At one time we had a full-time secretary [for] this depart-
> ment, [which also serves as a] regional library for two states.
> Well, that person left [two to three years ago] and the job was
> never filled. . . . See these? These are things I had to send out
> in the mail. I photocopied these; I word-processed them. Then
> I carried them three flights down to somebody who has a
> laser printer, which I don't have, and then I carried them
> back up three flights to the photocopier. So a great deal of
> my time is spent in doing things which have nothing to do
> with what I'm being paid to do, and we can't afford a stu-
> dent. My student budget was cut 25 percent this year, even
> though I'm down by two staff members.

She concludes that "it's kind of a struggle all over. . . . Support positions often are the ones that don't get filled. People don't take them as seriously, but they make a difference in people's lives."

Brenda is also in a subject library with a small staff. She curtails certain activities in an effort to ease pressure and get primary work done. "I should be going to a lot of the meetings of the departments [I am liaison for], but I just really have not been able to fit that in." She also relies on a team environment around her: "I don't know how we'd survive here [without it]. . . . It's supportive, its flexible within the limitations of the work, and that helps us get our job done." A subject bibliographer, Elizabeth emphasizes that loss of staff and increased publishing in her subject areas means "I don't even see the books [I have]" ordered. This results in gaps in her own mental map of subject areas for which she is responsible. Elizabeth feels this diminishes the support she is able to give faculty and students. "I've grown farther and farther behind . . . So now I don't agree to serve on dissertation committees for all the students who want me, [and] I can't take the initiative in many of those [faculty] conversations that I [once] could." Fran adds, "I was here for three and a half years before I got a priority list put together—the sort of thing I used to do every quarter in my [previous library] position."

Inevitably, loss of librarians, support staff, and student workers takes its toll. Librarians in many units have reached that point. Brenda hears "a lot of talk about burnout among staff here and in the reference room." Fran says she and several others "are at the vacation ceiling, and we can't get two weeks in a row off, or three days in a row off . . . because if you're gone, somebody else then has to do some additional desk time or [other tasks]." In some units, the staff's involvement in necessary learning-teaching-training work means there is an increase in the number of hours when library users get information and data only from student workers. With an inadequate systems staff, Patti finds "either we don't [fix problems], or we have to ask the [university] computer people, 'Would you please help us do this?' And we're not their highest priority, we don't pay their salaries, so we're begging them to help us. And that's no way to run a library systems function." Judith stresses, "There are people who think you can just sit around all day and read books, but it's very—, just overwhelming, swamping, demanding. That's the downside of [my job]. And a feeling that I can never get unchained from my desk—I've got so many things to do." She talks about attending a stress management workshop, and its aftereffects:

> They gave us this test to see how stressful your job was. And the most stressful job was 100 percent; I got 96 percent. . . . There were questions like: "I have to go to other departments and ask people there to do things but they don't really know what I do." Well, I do that all day long. "I have many dead-lines, sometimes they all fall at the same time." Oh, yes, that's me. . . . I did make some changes in my life. I started doing some things that I like outside of work. . . . I started to say to myself, I have tenure. I'm an associate professor, if I botch this up, they can't fire me. It's amazing how good that can make you feel.

Other librarians "learn to put stuff on hold" (David) or do clerical work at home rather than take more time away from primary work. Overall, there is a feeling that regardless of how the library is perceived, "there isn't a lot of acknowledgment [by the institution] that you work in the library or did a good job on something, made a contribution" (Karen).

In a sense, the bureaucratic aspect of MIRI-U is more comforting than another way in which the institution is perceived by these librarians—through the combined lens of politics and culture. Lee G. Bolman and Terrence E. Deal (1997) consider the structural framework of an organization to be one of its most overt characteristics. They find that employees seem to easily rationalize the existence of rules, regulations, and how decisions are made. However, they note, employees generally have a much more difficult time dealing with an institutional culture that includes a strong political orientation. Seeing their university as an arena in which different interest groups compete for power and scarce resources, and where conflict, negotiation, and compromise are part of the norm, disturbs many individuals. At MIRI-U, most librarians feel they have come to see the competitive and power elements of politics as regular parts of their organizational life and as normal parts of academe. But they do not like to focus on such aspects and consider these elements absolute constraints. Judith speaks for almost all the librarians when she says:

> [What's] constraining are things that have to do with office politics and organization politics, and institutional politics. . . . Sort of people jockeying for power and position and power building, you know. And that's always been there. . . . I guess I have a finite amount of patience [with] it.

A MIRI-U alumna, Sandy remarks on how she resolved a question about coming back into such an environment when she moved from a corporate library to MIRI-U:

> When I interviewed for this job, one of the people on the committee just said, "Are you really ready to come back to the politics here?" And it struck me that at least in [this] political situation, they are assuming that everyone is bright enough [to handle it,] and everybody's in there doing something—even if they are doing some destructive things. So I said yes, I would come back to the politics.

Bolman and Deal (1997) go on to point out that all organizations have assumptions about values, beliefs, behavioral norms, and artifacts. And Harrison M. Trice (1993) notes that when such assumptions are given meaning through individual and organizational actions, they ultimately create a specific culture. With repeated use, the assumptions slowly drop out of employees' consciousness but continue to influence individual and organizational decisions, attitudes, and behaviors. They become part of the language of the organization—the underlying, unquestioned, but virtually forgotten, reasons for "the way we do things here" (Berger and Luckmann 1966; Ford 1975). Those who have worked at other universities characterize the "culture" at both MIRI-U and the library as rather bleak and uncaring. Mary describes MIRI-U as "a much tougher place to break into" than her previous university:

> I can attribute that, first off, to the age of the employees [and] fewer women who are middle and upper management.

... People have been here longer, they seem very seasoned, they've seen a lot of things come and go, a lot of people come and go. . . . People are settled here in a way that they weren't settled at [the other university].

As "the library is a microcosm of the university" (Jan), librarians share MIRI-U's culture. For example, Chris is relatively new to the university. She observes that "it's hard for new people, I think, when there's no effort to kind of socialize them into the system." She wonders if part of the lack of socialization and mentoring is because most of the librarians "have not worked at other places maybe, or have not necessarily been newcomers all alone at a place." She adds, "A lot of people here...went to library school together, started working about the same time, which is not what happens now. Just one person comes in, not very often, but kind of alone."

One result of such a culture is this statement from a librarian who has spent about six years at MIRI-U:

The one thing I always thought I would feel when I was in a professional position was a certain loyalty to the organization, to the institution. And I've never really felt that here. . . . I think partly because I don't feel like it makes much difference to the institution whether or not I stay. . . . I keep kind of hanging on thinking the more I put into it, something will be there.

The Library System

Physically, MIRI-U's library is arrayed over several buildings and, within each building, into discrete departments, offices, and collection stack areas. A number of physical changes occurred over the past five to ten years, including:

- moving the HSS reference desk and adding an information desk;
- removing the science information desk because of budget cuts;
- moving science-related catalogers to science library;
- relocating various subject libraries and archives on and off campus;
- merging some departmental subject libraries into science and HSS

• moving individual librarians either nearer to or farther from the materials with which they do much of their work;

• accepting responsibility for a data center, and subsequently relocating it to HSS.

Plans are now under way to bring more HSS subject-related libraries into closer physical proximity with each other, and the medical librarians are considering rearranging service locations. There is also discussion of relocating several disparate archival units to a single building. The central library administration offices are located in HSS.

Organizationally, the library system has the traditional pyramid structure common to academic libraries: a library director at the apex followed by assistant university librarians (AULs) and directors for technical, public, collection, medical, and other units (Hamlin 1981; Shiflett 1981). Each AUL is responsible for a number of related units. Various committees and teams operate within and across units. Formal administrative control follows the hierarchy.[1]

Structure: "We Go Centralized, Decentralized, Centralized, Decentralized..."

MIRI-U librarians are like many of the thinkworkers studied by Ralph Blankenship and colleagues (1977), the MOW IRT (1987), Abbott (1988), and Kanter (1990) in that, regardless of how many times there have been reorganization efforts, they continue to prefer decentralization of administration, and many prefer decentralization of location. Echoing Cohen and March's 1986 study of faculty and Hales's 1980 study of engineers, this decentralization preference is very strongly felt and valued. Galen understands this sentiment:

> When I first came [to MIRI-U], I was kind of appalled at the literal, in the sense of physical, separateness—the sense of not even belonging to this organization. Very much of a separateness, administratively and psychologically. [Over time,] I have begun to appreciate the value, to some extent, of the decentralized kind of environment.

Galen explains that if they must report to someone in central library administration, librarians want that individual to have experience with their particular kind of primary work. This is true regardless of a librarian's unit or location but is particularly felt among those located physically outside HSS, the library building that includes central administrative offices. As a member of the science library, Galen uses a previous attempt at organizational centralization to make this latter point:

> We fell under the sway of people who live in the [HSS] library but have responsibility for us. . . . We got the worst of both worlds. We're separate, but we don't have the autonomy or the power to act separately the way some of the other [outside] units do. . . . [Working with] something that is physically separate, functionally different, and unfamiliar to [our current administrator] is just too much for anybody.

A member of the medical library staff in yet another library location, Patti agrees with the need for decentralization:

> Patti: One of the strengths of [this library] is that we have been sort of semiautonomous.
>
> Interviewer: Would you want to be closer in association with the rest of the library system?
>
> Patti: Not any more than we are. No, I think it's fine. We're close enough.

Librarians value decentralization because it lets them run their own unit—making decisions directly affecting their work and that of their unit colleagues. Exemplifying findings by Blankenship (1977), Eliot Freidson (1986), Edward E. Lawler (1992), and others who study professionals, MIRI-U librarians expect to be fairly autonomous, self-directing, and self-managing. Within subject libraries, they also believe unit-level decision-making benefits library users. Across the library system, there is a sense of community felt within various units that the librarians attribute in some measure to decentralization of organization and location.

At the same time, they recognize some weaknesses in a decentralized physical, administrative, and psychological structure. Mary sees the latter as a barrier that has led to "too much factionalism . . . We don't have an environment that lends itself to a comprehensive approach." Tony notes it is easy to ignore reporting lines "because [the intervening layer] doesn't do anything for me. If I want anything in the way of a budget decision, [for example,] I go directly to the head. It's ridiculous to stop in the middle."

In large research libraries, subject specialization frequently results in many physically separate collections, which can contribute to isolation and confusion about "belonging"—regardless of building location. Witness Michele, whose subject library recently moved into HSS near the central administrative offices. She still feels:

> We don't fit in any one place. We're not a service [about which administrators can easily say], Oh, well this is a fee-based service, or This is a this kind of service,' or It's that kind of service. They don't really know what it is, so kind of like they grab at the part that they understand. . . . Shifting physical places has probably made it a little harder for the library to ignore me. Because they trip over me a few more times, . . . I kind of turn into a person rather than Who?

Fairly new to a specialized unit also located in HSS, Lynne finds it previously "had been pretty much left to its own devices...so there were all sorts of little procedures, you know, that sort of got longer and longer." Since she came in as unit head, "We have certainly streamlined an awful lot of things." Lynne is also typical of many subject librarians when she notes that getting online in MIRIUCAT increases contact with users and strengthens ties to other library staff. This sentiment is echoed by Mark, in a different library building, who sees the relationship between his archival unit and the rest of the library system as "in some ways *in* it, but not *of* it":

> Until ten years ago, we were located off campus . . . and there, we were really out in our own world. And we consciously sought to get moved onto campus. . . . That was sort of a survival tactic—that we were going to be out of sight, out of mind if we weren't more integrated with the library and with the rest of the local campus. If we didn't matter to anyone here, no one was going to advocate for us at the next

retrenchment round. . . . The attempt to fold us into MIRIUCAT has been real useful.

MIRI-U librarians always want some ties to exist throughout their system. Engaging in committee work and becoming members of project teams are two common ways to make such connections. These functional and, practically speaking, social groupings allow them to share information, work standards, and power, and to feel part of a "community of practice" (see Lave and Wenger in Darrah 1996).

The librarians rate the importance of a committee by its relationship to their primary work: The closer its responsibility is to a work responsibility, the more acceptable—perhaps even valuable—it is to serve on that committee. Most important are those that directly affect primary work by virtue of the process, product, or policy they address. For example, librarians focusing on catalog work give more value to serving on a catalog-coordinating body than on a committee where catalog aspects are only one of several charges. For most librarians, the committees least valued are those having to do with the library in an organizational or administrative sense, such as the Library Council or a faculty personnel committee. Involvement is "citizenship duty" (Mark). Librarians will prefer almost any primary work activity over committee work, and when primary work increases they "don't serve on as many committees or go to as many meetings" (Susan).

MIRI-U librarians see this activity as part of work life because it serves as a two-way communication channel across the library and because "we are expected to do some library service as part of our performance [as librarians]" (Nancy). It also ensures that one's unit or primary work area has a voice in policy-making. "Some committees *are* important," stresses Patti, adding that she is likely to volunteer for, or campaign to be elected to, a committee where "I think there's not enough input from the sciences; [where] I think we need a bigger voice."

Committee work is rarely enthusiastically sought, and when librarians agree to it, they want the activity to take as little time as possible. Nancy speaks for most when she says, "When I work on a committee, I'm pretty practical in looking for the practical answer to something." Galen is typical when he puts committee service into a "miscellaneous" category of work. Although librarians acknowledge that time varies with task, most believe they spend close to 25percent of their work time on some kind of committee task—without including preparation and debriefing time.

MIRI-U librarians respond more positively to membership on teams. These are self-directed—distinguishing them from committees, which are generally charged with reporting or recommending to an administrator at a higher organizational level. Team members commonly have "day-to-day responsibility for managing themselves and the work they do with a minimum of direct supervision and [they] typically handle job assignments, plan and schedule work, make production and/or service-related decisions, and take action on problems. [Members] are jointly responsible for whole work processes" (Fisher 1994, 243; see also Hackman and Oldham 1980). At MIRI-U, the librarians find less organizational hierarchy and bureaucracy, more shared decision-making, and increased informality and collegiality among team members than among committee members. Although teams most frequently serve as task-oriented working groups focusing on specific problems or projects, a few library units have become entirely team oriented. Nancy notes, for example, that "our unit has been marked by cooperation as a team since [our unit head] took over six years ago. It is one of the best things about our unit." Recently, the number of across-unit teams has increased. A cross-unit project commonly has "an overall committee [and] the membership changes with whoever is working on [the project]" (Elaine). Several librarians feel they now work best "in a team environment or a group" (Mary) and would agree with Chris's sentiments:

> I'd like to see more teamwork involved [in the library], and teamwork that kind of crosses functions, too—not just technical services, but public services. I don't necessarily feel like I want to be a cataloger doing reference work, [but] I want to know what's going on out there. . . . There are some informal things going on now, but it would be nice to see that developed more.

To some degree, the increase in teams results from the torrent of library and business literature that promotes moving from hierarchical to team-based structures. It also reflects the reality of lateral organizations and the demands of a learning environment (see Zuboff 1988; Senge 1990; Rousseau and Wade-Benzoni 1995).

Administering and Managing

MIRI-U librarians do not aspire to administration—in part because they like their primary better, and in part because they view administrative work as secondary and negative. Nancy is representative; she finds herself "shying away from administration at just about every point." Corresponding to faculty views of university administrators, some librarians do not see library administrators as librarians. This is inferred in Karen's response when asked What would you do if you were *not* a librarian?: "I'm not sure. I'm not sure I'm drawn to administration at this point. And moving up would be different—although I've had changes before." Patti summarizes librarians' views when she says, "The bottom line is I don't want to be an administrator, and so I sort of let them do their things and [they] let me do mine."

When librarians talk negatively about administrators and administration, they mean those at the highest levels in the library hierarchy—division heads, assistant and associate university librarians, and university librarians; they exclude unit heads. Chris, who functions as head of a team within a unit, draws the proverbial line in the sand when she talks of distinctions in the organizational hierarchy: "those who are division heads and those who are not." The latter are called "our unit head," "boss," or "supervisor"; some function as colleagues. And although not true in every unit, in general, librarians view favorably their own unit head and perhaps those one level higher. Mary and Nancy have the same unit head and articulate some valued characteristics of such librarians:

> Mary: My unit head is wonderful. She's been incredibly supportive and interested, and offered me a great deal of flexibility.

> Nancy: Our unit head is very understanding and has a good ·attitude, and we respect her highly. No one says negative things about our unit head. . . . She shares with us when she has problems about doing something or has hesitancy about her way of doing something. She tries to get feedback from us. It's a very open environment. And it's not highly con-

trolled. She expects us to be professionals on the job, and I think we live up to that.

In another unit, Patti demonstrates connections between a positive view of a unit head and feelings of autonomy: "My supervisor is wonderful because she gives me the autonomy to try new stuff. Now if I think it's a little risky or it's going to involve money, I'll talk to her. But I can't remember if she's ever said no. So it's great." Fran agrees that it is a welcome situation to have a boss with whom one has "pretty straight-forward relations." Such individuals engender "a lot of respect" (Rose).

For many librarians, administrators develop negative images as a result of actions ranging from not knowing individual librarians in units reporting to them to having a reputation for forgiving faculty almost any and every violation of library policy. In general, public service administrators are seen as more supportive of librarians than those associated with technical service work. The latter are frequently characterized as "not good people person[s]" (Brooke), and as being more process than service oriented. MIRI-U librarians evaluate administrators on the basis of how frequently librarians' input is sought and incorporated into decisions, by how much administrators know about what librarians do and need, and by how they support librarians.

Uniformly, MIRI-U librarians dislike administrators who want things their own way and who exclude librarians from decision-making. The fundamental issue is whether control over primary work is to be exercised by administrative personnel or the librarians closest to the work (Freidson 1986; Trice 1993). Galen cites problems with decisions about, for example, "what databases are going to go on the OPAC, or very directly relevant things to our job. I don't think we have the input to see that our needs are served, and so decisions get made and we're not consulted. It does have a very real effect on how we can work." Wariness of top-down management is illustrated when Margaret discusses TQM efforts, noting that "I think it has to be applied by 'believers' to work. And I'm not sure in [this library system], where it's a matter of the top administration saying, Well, you will do TQM, that all the people [who] are involved are necessarily really on board." And as Brenda tactfully suggests, "[Although] there still has to be some hierarchy so that decisions are made and things progress, I think actual input from the people who are doing the actual work . . . should have a little more value."

Worse than exclusion is feeling that one's input has been ignored after being requested. Several librarians comment independently on this irritation:

> Mary: Things get studied or played with or mapped around a lot, and then they disappear. So you put your heart into something that's special to you, and it's gone. . . . I've heard too many stories from too many people about being encouraged to work on this idea or that idea or this project, and that happens and then it's gone. Because something else has moved up as a priority or an urgent need or whatever.

> Tony: [A frequent question is,] Once this report gets into the hands of the administration is the administration going to act on it? . . . [Or will] they just kind of slowly let it trickle away until people forget about it? And it'll be another exercise in futility.

> Patti: A lot of it is they think they know what's best . . . maybe we who work the reference desk know something and they should listen. And the same with circulation, maybe they know. And there's some [inclusion]. But a lot of it's token, too. We will get asked for our opinion, and then it's ignored.

Most irritating are situations when librarians in one area are not involved in an administrative decision made on behalf of those in another, and yet the result affects both groups. Database decisions engender the most complaint, especially several purchased for HSS and loaded onto the systemwide MIRIUCAT; they were not helpful to users of the science or medical libraries. From the medical library, Patti says in an exasperated tone that "the search software we could have gotten would have been better. But they didn't ask us. They just did it."

Librarians believe many administrators do not know what those not reporting directly to them do or need. Nancy offers the example of when she was new to her unit and found that a central library administrator "did not realize that we only had two manual typewriters down here. I said, 'Do you realize that?' [He said,] 'No! I never heard of it.'. . . . [Then someone in the library office] signed off and we got computers." On a broader level, many archive and subject librarians feel administrators "really don't have a great understanding of what we do so they let us alone. And as long as we don't do anything too stupid, we're alright" (Elaine). As someone primarily doing catalog work, Andy muses that "I think a lot of administrators imagine the catalog as something that [is] very solid and right." He adds, "and it's just not right. It breaks down every day [because] things that were right yesterday [in the world] aren't right today." In the medical library, Sandy believes central library administrators "assume that our job is just like their job when they were reference librarians. And it's just not true. I mean, journals are so much bigger for us, and currency [of issues] is such a big deal. . . . It's sort of surprising to me to realize that the administration doesn't get that." Brenda sums up general sentiment on this issue by saying "decision-making originates from [central library administration], and I don't know that they're very in tune with what we're doing on a daily basis." And Sandy thinks "it's their job to . . . find out [what we do, although] certainly they shouldn't be expected to know it just from osmosis."

Librarians also evaluate administrators on the basis of how the latter support them. When speaking of division heads and above, MIRI-U librarians tend to emphasize failings, as when Michele talks of having to change locations because another campus unit wanted her space: "Nobody even went to fight. Nobody even really went to the battle. There were bigger fish to fry someplace else. We lost out." Most of the time, "support" is meant in personal terms, such as when Patti sees administrators "erring too much on not defending, not being supportive enough of the library staff if there's a conflict between...the public and the staff." Or, when Michele grumbles that "I have to remind them every year that I am the university's representative to [a national association] and therefore you guys are supposed to pay for it. . . . It's this constantly having to remind them."

The librarians do grant administrators some positive attributes. Galen believes "people with more of an administrative background can learn enough of the technical side [of work] to do what needs to be done or to find people to do the really nitty-gritty easier than you can take someone who's inclination is [in details] and teach them the big picture." In commenting on central library administrators being biased toward librarians with whom they share the HSS building, Patti thinks there might be merit in locating them in the proposed new archive facility: "I think it might help because it would be more neutral territory." But, regardless of where they are located, she appreciates that they "do all that administrative junk that I don't want to do." And Chris sees value in restructuring the library into a team-operated organization where administrators could also be team members:

> You may still need someone who's ultimately responsible for the work, kind of like "the buck stops here" or whatever. If that person is not doing the work or [is] not part of that team, there's a different sense of responsibility for it, I think. [As a team member,] it's also my work too, it's not just being responsible for other people's work.

Although MIRI-U librarians believe they and administrators would benefit if the latter regularly did some unit-level work, there is one task that almost all librarians would place off-limits. A number of years ago, library administrators approved creating an information desk in HSS to help users with questions about where something or someone is physically located and with questions relating to MIRIUCAT. Given its close location to a large cluster of MIRIUCAT terminals, the desk's best support goes to that increasingly complex online system, and anyone with outstanding catalog and database skills provides extremely valuable service to such users. Everyone who commented on the information desk strongly believes that catalog support should come first and directional assistance should be given as needed.

Volunteers, including several administrators, regularly staff this area. Administrators see the time spent as a way of demonstrating that the user is most important in the library. In contrast, librarians see having administrators there as a bad use of salary money, a demeaning image of the library and librarians, a waste of time that could be better spent on other matters, and irrelevant to the needs of both users and librarians. Much more preferable, they think, is administrator contact with librarians' primary work. Sandy summarizes the difference between appropriate and inappropriate unit work in her description of an administrator who works a regular shift each week at a reference desk:

> A lot of it is just a move of goodwill on her part and a move on her part to make sure she kind of keeps the pulse of things. I think it's wonderful. And I know that some of the administrators over at [HSS] work on the information desk, which is, Here's the bathroom. I mean, it's not the same as answering reference questions. I think if they did, if they were more in touch, it would make a big difference. I feel like the fact that [our administrator] works at the desk really changes her perceptions about what is important in the library.

Administration is generally described as containing more formal authority and a wider scope for action than management. Presenting a common view, G. Edward Evans (1983, 25) believes that "administrators establish fundamental patterns of operation and goals for an organization, while managers primarily carry out the directions of the administrators." MIRI-U librarians, who frequently oversee work of other librarians, support staff, and student workers, would resent such an approach. The librarians acknowledge that they feel somewhat differently about managing—perhaps because they do a lot of it. Yet, even though accepting it as part of their work, they downplay its significance. They see "managing" always in terms of a list of tasks that are considered secondary rather than primary. For Patti, who coordinates a reference area, it is "just making sure everything at reference is OK: scheduling, the computers are working, the books are on the shelves, it's staffed, new things are installed when they're supposed to be installed." Those with subject library or archive management responsibilities view it with a broader lens:

> Peg: Managing the library is the first obligation. And that means acquiring books, maps, and manuscripts . . . getting them cataloged. . . . You['ve] got to run the place, making sure of everything, the personnel, the budgeting, and all that.

> Mark: Selection and acquisition negotiation with creators of materials. . . . Then what we refer to as "appraisal". . . . I can't do it always myself, but I'm entirely involved in that here, and probably spend as much time as anything on reference and outreach, the interpretation . . . and then the general management of the unit.

Librarians also downplay the need to supervise others, except when it refers to training new staff or student workers. Supervising usually is seen negatively because it is associated with "all the paperwork junk you have to go through" (Pat) and "because now and then someone will have to be talked to about something" (Sandy). In addition, Brooke notes, it is time-consuming—meaning "I have less time to do cataloging than I would like." She regrets that people who need supervision "need a lot of supervision . . . checking over, reviewing, or editing folks' work, spot checking—takes a lot of time." Chris, also a cataloger, says, "I don't like supervising in the sense that people supervise here. I don't like keeping track of people's time. I don't mind training and evaluating work, but then I think it's the individual's responsibility to do what they [sic] need to do to get the work done." Andy strikes a balance between positive and negative characterizations: "Sure, I'm not keen on supervising, evaluations especially, [but] I accept it as a necessary part of the job. . . . It's good to be using my skills to enable other people to work."

Communication

This combination of disliking administration, tolerating management, liking decentralization, and yet supporting some degree of committee and team activities points to strongly held values about the need for an inter-unit and systemwide communication web. For these librarians, communicating is sharing knowledge or information, most frequently to inform decision-making. One example illustrates their emotional reactions to the topic of communication. Several years ago, the library system changed from the Dewey Decimal to the Library of Congress (LC) classification system and soon afterward closed the catalog for conversion to an online system. Reference librarians remember feeling irate during that period. They felt there was insufficient discussion with, and understanding by, catalogers on the impact on reference librarians and users as both faced LC call numbers on books, but Dewey numbers on existing catalog cards. When one part of the library system felt another part was not listening to its concerns, the result was loss of trust and weakened communication linkages.

Communication of library business is regularly carried out one-on-one, as well as within units, across units, and within committees and teams. In some measure, librarians even use social settings to discuss business issues. They have many forms for communicating—most frequently, oral and e-mail. Oral communication is commonplace. Margaret describes daily meetings with members of the unit for which she catalogs as "one way that we communicate" on a variety of topics. Nancy finds e-mail is "taking the place of all the phone calls that we used to make to each other." Library administrators have developed a weekly online "memo" that goes to everyone in the library system. Use of formal memoranda varies greatly among units. For Patti, informal lunches or coffee breaks are places where "you pick up on a lot of what's going on—and not only in your own department. [But] it's not the way one should do all one's communication in an institution. . . . For people who aren't involved in [the informal ways], you've got to be a little more formal."

There is agreement that good communication reduces psychological distance throughout the library system. But "good communication" is ill-defined. Essentially, MIRI-U librarians believe it exists when they are informed about everything they believe they need to know in order to do their work. The librarians measure this, to some degree, by how much they feel a part of a single community of librarians, which is akin to Lave and Wenger's idea of a "community of practice" (Darrah 1996). In such communities, all members participate regardless of whether they are central to the topics under discussion. At MIRI-U, this form of community currently appears weak. The librarians stress that communication avenues and efforts are insufficient across the system and believe one result is a decrease in their own effectiveness. This is especially felt by librarians who see themselves on the system's periphery—that psychological place where "I always felt like I was an odd man out and did not have any information: 'Please, give me some!'" (Karen). Many believe the most difficult aspect of attaining a high, consistent level of good communication at MIRI-U is in getting the library administration "to have any basic idea of what information everyone could use. They just don't seem to think things affect people and [items] are just sort of passed over. And then [the administration] is surprised when people react negatively" (Karen). Librarians are like most people functioning in a system where they depend on each other to fulfill work goals: They do not like to be surprised and they want to be involved. Weak communication links lead to frequent surprises and high frustration levels.

MIRI-U librarians believe communication must improve—regardless of how satisfied they are with what they now receive. Knowing about everything that might affect them means, they insist, not after even a tentative plan or decision is reached but, instead, as things are being thought about and developed. True to their sense of autonomy and responsibility for their work, librarians want some degree of involvement from the thinking stage forward. They particularly do not like "trying to deal with the problem after it's been put into place" (Karen). Using a very practical example, librarians want to know that a report has been received, that it has been read, that their comments were considered by those to whom they were submitted. On most issues, they want to know why choices were made—regardless of the topic. In the abstract, "we each have our own little territories and we work autonomously" (Elizabeth). Without good communication, boundaries get drawn, effectiveness decreases, and interactions between individuals or units become "the Mongols attacking the walls" (Pat).

Relationships

Across their university and library system, MIRI-U librarians seek positive, supportive relations. Collegiality and employment status are the two chief means through which relationships are either strengthened or weakened.

The term *colleagues* is applied to those with whom librarians feel the closest while at work. These relationships "provide the employee with friendship, social activities, and the support necessary to engage in the work activities of the organization" (Czander 1993, 350). According to Willliam M. Czander, colleague groups provide an emotional bond that performs three functions: managing implusivity at work, providing for self-esteem regulation, and ensuring a psychological safety net. MIRI-U colleagues see things alike regardless of primary work, serve on committees and teams together, and support each other. Within units and primary work areas, librarians strive "hard to develop a sort of collegiality" (Judith). In her journal, Nancy describes one person in her unit as a colleague "for as long as I have been here. We work well together." She describes the smoothness with which the two of them pick up each other's ideas and follow the same flow of action and thought in their approach to tasks and commitment to work. Andy illustrates this same sense of shared meaning when he talks of how satisfying it is to find consensus in decision-making: "It's not enough for me to know that I did [something] right and that users think it's right. I'd much rather know that colleagues in the same kind of decision-making process that I am [in] came to the same conclusion." Chris, also a cataloger, finds it helpful to go "see the places and talk to the people who are using these materials." Three times a year, Sandy, a medical librarian, arranges "lunch and a visit to the libraries of all the science folks. And we're including everybody that . . . works science reference."

Those doing the same primary tasks have the strongest shared meanings and thus the greatest sense of common bonds. Most frequently, MIRI-U librarians describe colleagues in their units as "a group of people [who] work together very smoothly" (Nancy). Patti concurs, noting that although the librarians in her unit are "a very competitive staff, fortunately [it is] not among ourselves, or rarely among ourselves. I mean, there are little things, you know, and there's gossip everyplace and stuff. But overall, I think the cooperation is very good." This sense of collegiality is sometimes apparent in librarians' frequent use of plural pronouns, such as Elizabeth's description of how her unit evolved: "We reorganized and we made a subject bibliography unit. We reorganized the clerical support work. And we said we will require [librarians] to come in with advanced degrees." Colleagues support each other. Although she substitutes *team* for *colleagues* in her conversation about reference work, Brenda illustrates this point:

> Frequently, there are unreasonable [users] . . . and having
> that support really helps. I don't know how we'd survive here
> if we didn't have a team environment. If there was a lot of
> interdepartmental conflict, I think it would be just extremely
> difficult to do the work. One of the things I like about this

particular job is the department environment because it is supportive, it's flexible within the limitations of the work, and that helps us get our job done.

Reference is not the only kind of work where there is "a lot of consulting back and forth among ourselves" (Fran). However, it is clearly one where necessary collaboration on tasks fosters collegiality of a sentient, or bonding, nature. In the more private areas of catalog and collection work, psychological distance between colleagues increases. Andy finds "normal work routines don't put me out there where I can ask [other catalogers] questions easily. I do go ask questions sometimes and interact with them. But it's—, you know, we don't work as a team." Chris agrees, noting that "cataloging full-time here means pretty much sitting at your desk all day." And although Margaret likes cataloging precisely because it allows her "to do things that I can do on my own," she feels she has developed collegiality with librarians in the separate subject library for which she catalogs.

Librarians located in different units or with different primary work feel collegiality develops as they collaborate on cross-unit tasks. As a subject bibliographer, Judith conveys this when she talks of connecting with a reference librarian about a project that "we'll probably do sort of jointly." Here, work activities rather than location or shared meanings serve as the defining component. However, the unit is still the strongest element:

> There are extra-departmental or extra-unit or interdepartmental connections that people have. Probably based on areas of interest, language skills or a particular research background, [they] do get together. But mostly, I see people from the subject bibliography unit with people from the subject bibliography unit, and people from administration with people from administration. (Mary)

When not many in the library system share primary work with a librarian and cross-unit activities are few, colleagues come from elsewhere. Michele's colleagues tend to be at other academic institutions. Meeting with them, she finds, "is like suddenly being part of a group of people where everybody understands what you're talking about, the issues that you're dealing with. You get that group together and they never want to leave. I mean, it's just like one big family. We don't want to leave each other." At MIRI-U, she finds her colleagues to be:

> the people that I find it most interesting and stimulating to deal with: archivists [who] deal with electronics, or people who are really talking about the implications of electronic information dissemination. . . . People who are at that cutting edge of working with hypertext and other forms of access. And those [who] are dealing with the real high-end research with numbers or with text.

Geographic decentralization can also lead to lack of communication and a diminished sense of collegiality. Karen notes that although "I work for a great group of people in the library," physical distance means "there are lots of people that I've never met, that I don't know." And explaining that subject bibliography offices are spread throughout the library system, Elizabeth sees advantages to being "right next to people." This is echoed by Judith, who feels that "even though I enjoy being autonomous, I really like having colleagues close at hand that [I] can talk to and interact with. . . . I think [our locations] hold us back...from really having a sense of community. [We] don't have that sort of give and take that I really would appreciate."

MIRI-U colleagues support each other, even when they are in different units or different buildings. Tasks draw them together, as when three reference librarians and a subject bibliographer collaborate on a user-oriented online product. Committee work also can be "a challenging cooperative venture" (Nancy). And Tony senses that involvement in one such group is leading to "developing all sorts of new skills that we didn't have before, like how to run focus groups, how to listen to others, to talk to people. We think that's going to be valuable." Being collegial means helping "a colleague who happened by and was stressed out" (Nancy). It means taking up the slack when a unit colleague goes on research leave or recognizing that others "can't do their job right [if] I didn't do mine right" (Margaret). It means responding positively to requests for assistance from someone in a totally different library area "because we've always had a good relationship. . . . He understands what we're doing enough, and I understand what he's doing enough, that whatever he eventually comes out with, we can make it work" (Michele). Colleagues, regardless of tasks or work areas, give librarians that emotional bond that says "we're in it together, they can rely on me and I can rely on them. That kind of tacit, 'We're getting there.' Maybe I'm making it up, but I don't think so" (Mary).

Collegiality, however, can be sharply curbed by one factor that the librarians cite more than any other:

> There are all of these classification distinctions. . . . There are civil service librarians here, faculty service librarians here, there are academic professionals, and there are all these temporary people who have one-year reappointments. And people get treated differently. There are different rules. (Karen)

Classification status is a complicated and divisive issue at the university. It can affect who is considered a colleague, what communication is (or is not) received, and what becomes shared meaning about work. At one time, the university had three employment groups: clerical staff, faculty, and civil service. Employees hired as librarians (with or without a master's degree in library science) were part of a state civil service category. In the 1960s, MIRI-U allowed librarians with an MLS to attain faculty status if they met university-wide research and publication requirements. Librarians not interested in meeting, or not able to meet, those requirements retained their civil service standing. In the 1980s, the university decided librarians could no longer have faculty status, nor could they continue to enter the civil service track. It created a new classification for two groups: professional and administrative employees (P&A). Incoming librarians were classed as professional. Already employed librarians were allowed to stay in their existing classification (i.e., civil service or faculty), or they could switch to P&A status. Currently, unless hired solely under administrative assignment, entering librarians are classed as professional on either a continuing track (i.e., tenure-eligible) or an annual appointment track (i.e., not tenure-eligible). MIRI-U's library system has librarians representing all four arrangements: civil service, faculty, tenure-eligible, and annual appointment.

Some civil service–classed librarians have an MLS; others do not. This category now contains the fewest librarians. Its conditions of service, including vacation, sick leave, dismissal, retirement, grievance, and other rights and responsibilities, overlap but are distinct from, those of other employment classifications. Librarians with this status carry out the same tasks as those librarians in faculty and P&A classifications. Some are unit heads and supervise librarians and/or support staff and student workers. However, they appear to be ineligible for research leaves and some believe they are excluded by status alone from serving on specific library system committees. Fran notes that this classification was closed to librarians for a number of reasons, one being "because they are so similar to the assistant librarian in the P&A class that people from the personnel department looking at the job descriptions couldn't tell them apart." Aside from mandated university policies, decisions about whether and how to view and treat librarians in civil service classification are library and, more important, unit specific. Three examples illustrate a range of unit behavior and attitude. First, Nancy describes her unit head, who holds civil service status, as someone who "has terms that last maybe three years or something like that. We're such a happy group with her, actually, that we don't even know when one term ends and another begins." In this unit, librarians seem to make no distinction between civil service, faculty, and P&A librarians. In a second unit, Brooke, who has an MLS and civil service status, feels isolated:

> I do not go to librarian meetings—not invited to them in [this subject library]. I get the same voting rights as the P&A people, much to the chagrin of some people, but I'm not included otherwise. . . . According to [university] classification, we are considered "professional", but if you were to ask anybody [here] if we were included as professional, they would say no.

Librarians in this unit appear status distinguished. Finally, Fran does not have an MLS and holds civil service status. She responded to a question about whether her status makes any difference in her work or with whom she works, by saying, "No [it does not]. I think probably because I've been around long enough and [have] established some credibility." Librarians in this third unit minimize status distinctions.

Chris is untenured in the P&A classification. Speaking from a fourth unit area, she sums up the situation of unit attitude toward librarians with civil service status, especially those without the MLS:

> When I say "librarian", I tend to mean everyone who works in the library, and that is not accepted here. There's a real distinction. A librarian is here, at least in technical services, a person with an MLS degree. And that's kind of hard. I've never felt that kind of elitism about having a degree [at other libraries]. I just don't see the necessity for having that kind of distinction. But it is very much [the case] here. And at this point, it's so ingrained.

Elitism is often a function of how a librarian sees his or her work in comparison with what he or she thinks exists for librarians in another status category. Among civil service–classed librarians, many feel one's primary work is most important and should take precedence over other interests and activities. A librarian's value and sense of self is in the doing of the work. On the other hand, for faculty-classed librarians, doing one's library-related work does not have such precedence. Elizabeth remembers the announcement of "a university vice president who said, 'Librarians will meet exactly the same standards for faculty status, in terms of quantity and quality as do other faculty members.'" Because librarians still worked a five-day week, twelve-month contract, she adds, "In order to teach, we had to devise our own opportunities, and in order to publish, we were working all night and weekends." As Bob explains:

> You entered this hazardous area where you had to get tenure. You had to start publishing. You had to do all these things. . . . You actually went through the whole [tenure and] promotion process. And that means at this level of peer group and central [library] administration through the academic vice president, through the president, through the board of regents.

For faculty librarians, this sense of accomplishment and peer footing with other faculty throughout the campus carries the ever-present value of a patina—of something "grown" beautiful. Even after receiving tenure, being a faculty librarian means more than focusing on the work at hand. Rose describes what it was like to be in the faculty category in the 1970s: "We had collegial governance and a feeling that we shared a vision and wanted to do exciting things together. We really were colleagues."

Judith explains that in the 1980s, when the university sought to deny faculty classification to librarians, "We were extremely active, first of all in opposing it and then, when that battle was lost, in trying to make the P&A track something that did reflect the realities of the librarian's life— made them important, integral members [of the university]." She says that in the original draft of the P&A classification, "there was no job security. There were no expectations that any university librarian might be interested in research or publishing. There was nothing built into it to facilitate . . . term leaves, [etc.]." Indeed, Tony thinks a number of librarians did adopt the P&A status because they believed:

> If you transfer from faculty rank to P&A rank, then as you go up for promotion you wouldn't have to worry about having the same stress placed on you for research and publication as the faculty would. . . . You know what happened, of course. I mean, it was predictable. Once the librarians . . . sat down to write the standards for promotion, what did they write in? Research and publication!

Requirements for professionals in the final P&A document do parallel many faculty librarian requirements. For example, it is clear that although P&A-classed librarians believe the process toward gaining tenure is not a publish-or-perish situation, "we are expected to do professional things. And it's probably a good idea to publish something and, you know, get involved and those kind of things" (Galen). MIRI-U librarians in this professional classification do not seem to feel the severity of the process as much as faculty librarians believe *they* did, and tenuring decisions are focused at a library rather than an institutional level. Yet, several untenured P&A librarians indicated that colleagues encouraged them to engage in certain research, publication, and committee service activities because they would "look good on [my tenure] resume" (Sandy). A number of P&A librarians also like doing research. Karen, who is untenured, talks of a current study "on a topic that hasn't been done before." She believes that "[although] after continuous appointment I won't have to publish so much anymore, . . . you don't feel that you [can] be a good librarian without doing it." Indeed, tenured P&A librarians continue to take advantage of annual competitive professional development leaves. As Nancy notes, now "more and more people have asked for them . . . [so] you have to have a rather good proposal to even be considered."

In terms of focus, P&A-status librarians reflect a merger of civil service and faculty standing. Because job performance takes the place of teaching as a condition of service, they feel quite comfortable emphasizing primary work activities. And because they have disciplined themselves through six probationary years of research and committee activities, they expect to maintain a sense of professional identity beyond their primary work.

Finally, librarians who have annual appointments are in either administrative positions in the P&A classification or temporary/project professional positions funded on an annual renewal basis. Michele believes that:

> You're kind of betwixt and between on a lot of things. You don't have access to . . . professional development leave, sometimes [not] to professional development funds. You have to be the one who keeps an eye out that when [such] money is available, it is not worded in such a way that you fall through the cracks because you're not support staff and you're not professional staff.

Mary finds "betwixt" also means losing out on "a great deal of informal and formal support" built around the tenuring process. She frequently feels "out of the loop," in part because of status. Significantly, Brenda speaks for several such librarians when she notes, "I don't feel I have a regular job. . . . I feel less powerful. I feel less motivated to do long-term things because I don't know [if I'll] be here for three years or five years."

MIRI-U librarians thus live with what Nancy calls "a curious mix." It annoys them for several reasons:

- Some librarians have responsibilities that others do not have.

- Some have perks others do not have.
- Some seem always to be working "on task," whereas others are away doing "professional things."
- Some have more freedoms than others.
- Some are included in activities from which others are excluded.

Ultimately, for the librarians, irritations about status boil down to (1) needing to be recognized as a "librarian" for the work one does and (2) being treated "fairly" across all situations. For the university and the library as a whole, the various employment statuses create ruptures in the fabric of unit, cross-unit, and other types of working relations, which runs the risk of limiting productivity. Indeed, many theorists suggest that it is actually through the formation and viability of such formal and informal social groupings that the work of the organization gets done (see Czander 1993).

The Context of Work

Work meanings are affected by what goes on outside a librarian's primary work area. Whether in industry, academe, or a library, the larger work setting is generally composed of organizational groups (departments, units, teams) having some degree of the following: a hierarchy of authority, established goals and objectives relating to that unit's work, and a relationship with sub- and superordinate units. Members of a unit tend to exhibit a general set of shared values and beliefs regarding working conditions, rights, and responsibilities; and have conscious and unconscious expectations of each other and of individuals in related units (see Bolman and Deal 1991; Birnbaum 1988; Bergquist 1992). For MIRI-U librarians, the larger context of their university and library is seen as both supporting and constraining the conduct of their work. The feelings they have about the larger surroundings in which they practice primary work are guided by their perception of the motivations and behaviors of the university, of the library as a whole, and of their coworkers and colleagues. Each librarian acts on, and reacts to, these stimuli to arrive at his or her own sense of place within the holistic organization.

Regardless of the structure and ambience of their workplace and of concerns over institutional size, support, politics, and culture, the librarians seem proud to be associated with the university. They see their work with, and on behalf of, students and faculty as important and as demonstrating support for and belief in MIRI-U's educational mission and its scholarly and research reputation. "I have an investment here," Nancy says, but then she continues, "I want to feel that we're well respected; that we're doing a good job; that we're doing our part, you know; and that we're doing [it] well." Her sense of affective commitment to her work and place of work is representative of most MIRI-U librarians. She has a strong sense of identification and involvement with the library and, to a lesser degree, the university. She believes in the library's goals, has a willingness to exert effort on its and the university's behalf, and feels she is a member of both (Rousseau and Wade-Benzoni 1995). She also places demands upon the university and the library system: to be respected as a professional, to be supported as she fulfills her responsibilities, and to be given the autonomy and participatory involvements necessary to retain her positive motivation and intrinsic commitment to her work and workplace.

MIRI-U librarians' sense of life-at-work centers on their primary tasks, their unit, and their colleagues. These components form their basic work world. Within it, is "we"; outside it, it is "they," although the strength of this division depends somewhat on the topic under discussion. Thinkworkers, such as librarians, seem to especially value a decentralized organization (Zuboff 1988). Indeed, because their work is of a generally abstract nature (rather than rote), the library system's hierarchy seems always conflicted. Exemplifying Freidson's (1973, 1986, 1994) findings about professionals, whereas administrators see the need for advancing and preserving the integrity of the library system as a whole, the MIRI-U librarians see a compelling need to advance and preserve the integrity of their own specialized endeavors. The librarians would agree that they live within the adhocratic model proposed by Rousseau and Wade-Benzoni (1995); their view of administrators further conforms with this. They prefer administrators who are facilitators, who negotiate but do not command, who bring about a sense of organizational purpose and orderliness through interpretation and persuasion rather than imposition of decision. Librarians want involvement in decisions (including policy-making and governance), and more timely, frequent, and content-driven communication throughout the library system. They acknowledge that "there still has to be some hierarchy" (Brenda) but prefer an organizational structure as flat as possible, in part so that administrators better identify with the range of work done throughout the library system, even if they perform little of that work themselves.

The evidence gained thus far about perceptions of MIRI-U and its library system confirms the notion that a librarian's:

> willingness to take on the risks and rewards of creating and communicating explicit meaning is likely to be related to the character of his or her other social experiences, the psychological and communicative competencies that have been regularly emphasized, and the structure of the current social context as regards its capacity to invite or inhibit the individual effort to create meaning (Zuboff 1988, 205).

The complexity of such a work setting requires integrative mechanisms. Sharing interests and concerns with colleagues and coworkers helps a great deal. Shared meanings about governance, primary work, and the value of collaborative tasks connote community. These unifying work ethic elements help overcome status distinctions and a negative institutional cultural climate.

Zuboff (1988, 401) believes that "the demands of a learning environment can reduce the psychological distance between the self and the organization because active engagement in the social processes associated with interpretation requires more extensive participation of the human personality." We can take this to mean that for the librarians, the more library decision-making is a participatory act across functional and structural boundaries, the more engaged they become with coworkers at various locations and levels throughout their organization. Within their place of work, MIRI-U librarians continue to make their work central. In various ways, they exemplify the concept of "the active worker" (Hodson 1995): one who is an active agent in determining the very nature of work. And because they are thinkworkers within an adhocracy, it is not at all unusual that they tend to be distrustful of authority in general and of autocratic forms of administration in particular; that they want to participate in the design of the work setting as well as in decisions that affect them; and that, as shall be seen, they seek a "fit" that includes autonomy, growth, and personal satisfaction.

NOTE

1. As a result of a 1995–1996 librarywide reorganization process, this structure is now under review.

4. Expressions of Self: Values and Preferences

As part of making sense of work, MIRI-U librarians construct concepts to explain (i.e., give meaning to) their own and others' work-related tasks and activities. Some concepts have especially significant meaning for them. These expressions lack specific job associations such as reference or catalog or collection work; they also lack taken-for-granted, descriptive understandings associated with critiques of their library and university setting. As individuals, MIRI-U librarians may not easily or consciously articulate more abstract concepts such as being librarians, service, achievement, and choice. However, when their comments are brought together into conceptual terms, it is clear that, as a group, they vest such expressions with meaning beyond the ordinary, the every day. That is, they give such concepts highly positive significance and meaning (hereafter, significance-meaning).

Concepts emerge as the result of individual librarians assigning meaning to their own happenings and then associating with other librarians to socially construct (share) meanings (Ford 1975). When people act on the basis of meanings, those actions yield real, physical consequences. Roy F. Baumeister (1991) believes actions regarding work that carry this particularly strong bonding also carry subtle, generally covert implications and help establish a context for the more everyday tasks and activities associated with one's work. MIRI-U librarians articulate their significance-meaning concepts through what Seymour Epstein (1989) labels a "rational conceptual system." That is, they use conventional library words, jargon, symbols, and rules of logic to express the values and preferences they associate with particular library work concepts. This is in contrast to using what Epstein calls an "experiential conceptual system," which is inferring the existence of specific values and preferences from observation about one's own emotions and/or behavior. Espstein suggests that predominantly intellectually responsive individuals use the logical system, whereas those who are more affectively responsive use the experiential system. As seen earlier, MIRI-U librarians give strong positive values and preferences to their primary work and mixed-to-negative values and preferences to other activities within their library and university setting. The perceptions discussed in this chapter contribute greater dimension to each librarian's work identity.

On Being Librarians

The librarians have strong images of what it means to be a librarian. They are aware of the old stereotype of a middle-aged female in glasses who enforces quiet (Wilson 1982; Radford and Radford 1997). That image is not theirs, nor do they find it among most library users and campus colleagues. In her subject library, Patti finds that some users specify they want assistance from librarians rather than from student workers or support staff: "To find information, they know that those are the people who are supposed to be in charge of this place and that they have the most knowledge, the most experience. . . . So like you would ask for a physician, not a physician's assistant—because they're not quite the same." Galen finds that "a lot of [users] expect more of us than we can probably deliver, which may be counter to the stereotype. . . . I don't get the idea that they think we're just clerks." Yet, he adds, "You know, they do think anybody that works in a library is a librarian [including] the student . . . or the paraprofessional at the circ[ulation] desk." Musing on how users react to librarians doing reference work, Brooke says, "If you can find the answer to a question, you are the greatest thing on earth. If you can't—. Actually, there are occasionally some people who thank you profusely for trying the best you can. That's the best kind of client." She worries, however, that "we—as a profession—do not convey very well to our public that we are there to be able to help you find that information." Indeed, it seems to most MIRI-U librarians that academic users frequently miss what Andrew Abbott (1988) sees as essential abstract aspects of librarian work: diagnosis of immediate need, anticipation of future need, and control of information representation.

A subject bibliographer, Judith would agree with Abbott's characterization. She thinks that if user stereotypes of librarians are actually true, "I'm not the ideal librarian, because . . . when you read about librarians, they're supposed to be well organized and pay a lot of attention to detail. And every time I read one of those, I think I'm in the wrong field." Later, she comments:

> [You know] those studies about how librarians [are] sort of passive and detail oriented and organized? I know lots who are not. I always just thought that was one more ugly stereotype. But in truth, we're all human beings and so some librarians, I think, are always going to be passive and scared, and others are going to seize the day.

Representing many MIRI-U librarians, Sandy summarizes how she thinks users envision librarians in general and how she hopes that view will change:

> Everyone has this impression from the third grade: They know about Dewey Decimal, they can find a book in the school library. And I think they still look at public libraries and I think even academic libraries, as if "Well, if [I] took time and went in, [I] could probably do it. It's probably just the same. It would be real simple." And I think that as things get more complicated, [users] are going to realize—. Well, hopefully, we'll get a little more respect out of it and they'll realize that the organization of [information] is really a huge issue. I think the total disorganization on the Internet gives those people an appreciation for things that are organized.

Some librarians believe the Internet alone is not enough. Karen, for example, believes librarians continuously have to educate users about academic librarianship. Coming into a new subject library, she discovered that faculty thought her work and role did not (and should not) extend beyond the physical confines of her collection: "They felt 'she should be here 40 hours a week. . . . We should always be able to get her.' And I met with them and kind of explained it's a good thing that I get out and around." She believes they now understand "that I'm keeping [this] library out there where people are aware we're working hard . . . that I'm bringing them information. I have connections that I can [use]; I can get the things we need. In order to do that, I have to be out there working with other people. I have to do professional things."

Other librarians conclude that when users come to see libraries as technologically based information centers, they will more fully appreciate "what we know about classifying information and making it accessible" (Nancy)—points Abbott (1988) also makes about information professionals. In this vein, the librarians hope users will begin to see that librarians always had, and will continue to have, "a monopoly of organizationally relevant knowledge that provides them with considerable leverage over the transient client. They, like other professional employees, can control clients in part by restricting information on how to work the system and by keeping [clients] dependent" (Lipsky 1980 in Freidson 1986). For example, Patti suggests, users:

> are going to realize that more and more we're sort of the techie people, so I think that's going to be a big change. And [they will recognize] more that we're going to connect them to the information or show them how to get to it. We're not going to hand them the information. I think there's going to be too much of a demand to do that. . . . So [we'll] be more directing and educating. . . . I think they do realize that we know more than [they do].

Michele agrees, noting that some faculty are now approaching her as more of a partner: "I'm involved in people's research projects frequently from the early stages. You get faculty coming and [saying], 'I'm interested in this kind of issue. What kind of data is there out there? What can we work with?'" While ruminating about the disconnect between expectations of users and their image of librarians, Galen suggests that one change in the image will come about because librarians "certainly need to know what [various technologies] can do. They may not necessarily be able to do it themselves in a very technical way, but they need to understand the capabilities and that sort of thing, for sure." In fact, MIRI-U librarians ascribe some fairly specific characteristics to librarians, in general, and academic librarians, in particular:

> Galen: The most important thing is [a] really good broad background, general knowledge, for starters. . . . Certainly beyond just one discipline. . . . I think also just intellectual curiosity, interest in things, and willingness to keep up and broaden one's horizons to other things. I think a willingness to cooperate. Someone who doesn't have such an ego that they can't ask questions or are hard to ask questions of. Either way, but I think you need that kind of give and take, and willingness to share and to depend on [each other] as well—to interact. You learn a lot that way, and the public benefits [as] everybody has their special bits of knowledge.

> Judith: [Librarians don't] stop to think of themselves as sort of being agents of change. They're just putting [information] out on the network. And in fact, we're a tremendous agent of change. . . . Librarians tend to be forward-looking and interesting people.

> Shelley: Good librarians have a sincere interest and like what they're doing. Giving it their best effort—that's a competent best effort.

> Sandy: People skills. And I knew that librarians dealt with people, but I didn't realize how much they're called upon to deal with all different situations. [We] have really wonderful communication skills that people don't even recognize [we] do. I mean, patrons, crabby patrons, walk up and don't realize that the reason they go away not as crabby is that you

have spent a lot of time trying to— You know, like you didn't just take them and throw something at them because they were nasty. I think a lot of energy goes into that. I wouldn't have realized that [before becoming a librarian].

These images suggest some of what librarians would like users to see, as well as what they want in themselves and hope for in colleagues. Bob illustrates a particularly broad ideal of librarianship when he concludes that:

in reality, [librarians] can do anything. And nobody will believe that, but in reality if you've had library training, you've got the basics and most of the things you need. What you have to do is apply yourself, and whatever thing you go into you're able to do it. And it's really hard to get [librarians] to think that way. But they can shift jobs in the library. All it takes is a while to cross-train into whatever the new thing is.

A large number of studies on occupational preferences and choices finds there is a tendency for "persons with abilities corresponding to an occupation to choose that occupation" (Vroom (1964; 1995, 82). And indeed most MIRI-U librarians are academic librarians by choice, a few by chance (see appendix). Those who stay in this field do so because, as Nancy says, "the fit is good." When an individual integrates characteristics of a work role into her or his sense of self, a professional "fit" results. When that fit does not occur, the individual is "psychologically unable to join the organization and remains on the periphery" (Czander 1983, 305). Creating a fit with academic librarianship or within a particular library's setting is not necessarily a quick, conscious, or easy development. Brenda, for example, "didn't really have a big game plan" at first, but "I enjoy the university community and, you know, you're keeping up with what's going on in a particular field. In a large academic library, there are more resources than a small college. You're more in tune with the technology." Now she feels she will stay in a large, research library "just because there's more going on, there's more action." Michele is among those who firmly believe "if I weren't in an academic library, I wouldn't be in a library at all." She could conduct her numeric data work in other areas of a university, but in no other kind of library—she feels—than an academic one.

Sandy represents a more typical view: "I really wanted to work with an academic library. I [have] never worked anywhere but [in] academics my whole life except [once]. . . . If I would have been able to pick [any] job, it would have been this one." She adds:

> I really wanted to work someplace where I was not the only librarian or one of two or even one of three because I feel like there's so much to learn all the time. . . . So I wanted to work in a setting that was big enough. . . . I didn't leave [my faculty discipline] because I disliked it, I left it just because I found something I liked better. So it was fun to be able to come back and use the language I knew and [have] some background. . . . It's just I like being with people that are interested in learning all the time. I'm happy that I ended up in a profession where I'm expected to continue learning, [and where] to put it kind of bluntly, everyone here is overqualified for their job.

Patti muses over whether this kind of work is forever satisfying: "Ten years where I was, ten years here, and then something else? But for now, I can't think of a better place, which is a great feeling. You know, I feel sorry for a lot of people who don't have that now or who never have that—to be able to look forward to going to work. Kind of great."

Work satisfaction is, indeed, in the eye of the beholder. It is the end result of past occurrences and present-day realities (Czander 1993). Lynne, who moved into MIRI-U from public library work, illustrates this when she notes that in her current position:

> you get fewer people who are coming because they themselves are going to do something actively with the information, and more people who come because it's an assignment. . . . The other thing, of course, that hits you kind of like a brick when you come to a place like this is the absolutely endless bureaucracy. . . . People have asked me before [if I would make the change again], and I've just never really totally, totally answered it. Yeah, I guess I would. I think I probably would.

She bases part of her decision on finding it "so exciting being at a place like this where so much really neat stuff is going on" among both library colleagues and faculty. And she values, in particular, having a regional component to her work: "[That] was clearly a new and interesting challenge. It was a much bigger pond to play around in."

Karen's recognition of some positives and negatives inherent in being an academic librarian is also based on comparison with other work life experiences. She was in publishing before doing graduate studies in library and information science, and originally thought of public or corporate library work. She concluded, however, that "I also have a strong feeling that I have a special responsibility not just to service or professional achievement . . . but to work with other people." When she combined this sense with her quantitative background, interests, and a university climate, the fit was complete. However, she adds:

> [Although] I had more of an idea of what is involved than the general public does, I wasn't prepared to have to deal with conflict. I never expected to have people screaming at me because they, you know, had been fined . . . or strange people. All those things that are outside what people think about libraries. And I also don't think that I realized about all the challenges.

Now, after being in her subject library close to five years, "I can't imagine another type of work that would have sharpened my brain and skills like librarianship. It's a good match. I feel very lucky."

Almost all MIRI-U librarians believe that academic librarianship is their preferred profession. Only one or two can envision moving into some other work. A few think about public or school librarianship but find that the ambiance of the university and the nature of their primary work keep them pleased with their choice. Some, like Judith, find satisfaction in "supporting what the students and faculty [need]." Others who work directly with users would agree with Mary, who find, "almost every time somebody asks me a question, that I'm fully engaged in the process of trying to find the best thing or the best things in the most timely fashion." For Elizabeth, part of being an academic librarian means "integrat[ing yourself] into the place where you work in order to be important and in order to really make your work effective. In order to not get off doing your own little things and think they're important because you think they're important, but to have them tied in to what the organization does." Fran would go into academic librarianship again, even "as frustrating as it is" because of "the combination of dealing with things that are happening currently, dealing with a mix of public contact but not continually, and doing that at different levels. Trying to make the next time you deal with that same question better. . . . Identifying problems. [I enjoy] all of it."

For MIRI-U librarians, academic librarianship "is more than just a nine-to-five, and you drop it when you go home" (Patti). It is, suggests Bob, "a feeling for the system, not just your little job with its title." It is seeing "things the library needs to do" (Nancy). It is "keep[ing] the broad, the big picture in mind all the time" (Elaine). Being an academic librarian at MIRI-U, says Elizabeth, means "hav[ing] the possibilities of creative initiative...to be effective as a librarian." Or, as Shelley says, it is always "being on the 'bleeding edge'" of the future.

Professional Service and Personal Achievement

Librarianship has a long history as a service profession. Library thinkers from Pierce Butler (1951) to Michael H. Harris (1986) argue that librarians basically respond to user demands and prevailing societal or institutional canons. On the other hand, human resource theorists from Douglas McGregor (1960) through the MOW IRT (1987) stress that individuals in any line of work usually seek to accomplish more than a position or task requires. It turns out that MIRI-U librarians couple a service ideal with a strong sense of personal achievement.

In describing user-related work, MIRI-U librarians frequently talk of "helping," "assisting," "interpreting," or "mediating" users' information needs. They rarely use the word *service*, although the service concept is an established part of the literature of librarianship (Bunge 1980). Whether through direct or indirect interaction, MIRI-U librarians believe in helping and enabling users to connect with desired information. These two activities are distinct: *Helping* means direct interaction with users, and implies a shared operation; *enabling* provides users with the means for subsequent independent action. MIRI-U librarians appear to combine these concepts into a service ideal. They express that ideal in two ways that appear conflicted but actually are interconnected. First, librarians strongly believe that users who become independent of librarians for most of their needs ultimately make the best use of the library. This means that users know how to identify, access, and use relevant materials. Second, users always need to keep in touch with librarians because only the latter are charged with being current as to information resources, as well as with instructing users in how to fully manipulate a library.

Librarians carry out a service ideal in numerous ways, depending on their specific primary work and their own way of making sense of work. Sandy conveys a lot of the abstractness behind such an ideal:

> Before I was a librarian, I wasn't doing something that was sort of supportive and helpful—that was not ever part of my job before. And I think I like that part of it. That was a nice addition.
>
> Interviewer: Did you know that would be part of being a librarian?
>
> Sandy: Yeah. And I don't quite know why.

Galen may illustrate why Sandy knew such behaviors were part of librarianship. Galen's goal as a librarian is met through "giving people the information they need. . . . Teaching them how to use things, learn how to find their way around. . . . There's just a helping component." His ideal includes:

> bringing your knowledge and experience to bear, to help them, and to answer their questions . . . to know the collection, know the tools. . . . The downside, I think, is failing in something and then finding it two days later— and you don't have the guy's phone number.

Michele's ideal is that any library service or system be good enough "so I see fewer and fewer people [because] if they're looking up information, they can find it. . . . I mean, the whole point is to take yourself out of the loop so they can do it and have the information at their fingertips, and not to have to mess around with a human." She believes strongly that information "is not knowledge until it gets used and turned into knowledge, and that knowledge is applied." Her representation of information and knowledge finds support from Mark. In discussing connecting users to archival material, he explains that "we're providing access to information or data or something. But there's so much more to our soul in the sense that these documents really are a tangible link to the past." For him, the ideal of "match[ing] people's needs with available resources" is attained when "we've been struggling with all of this and finally hook the wire to the right pole—and the light goes on." Or as Rose phrases it, "What really makes me excited is when I can turn students on so that they get excited. . . . It's like a game going on where you try to recruit others (that is, students) into it."

This concept may be seen best through the extent to which librarians go to provide help and enablement to users—the vast majority of whom they do not know. Galen has an "outpost" by the science reference desk so users and staff do not have to trek to his office, which is on a different floor. For Fran, a service ideal is enacted as she moves from concerns over strengthening staff interaction with users to signage needs to the physical layout of her subject collection. Along the way, she invokes a teaching concept in showing users "what we're doing as we're doing something for them...[to] give them some scope, some additional information that will help them use the materials at a later date." All this, she says, is "because we're working for the patron." And users need not be affiliated with MIRI-U to be supported. In her journal, Nancy describes working overtime for a user calling from Illinois. Shelley comments on getting an e-mail from someone in California, who is seeking her particular help in finding out about a conference. She feels "I really need to answer this question" because "usually you don't get e-mail messages from people you don't know, so someone must have pointed me out for some reason."

For some MIRI-U librarians, helping and enabling also mean outreach on campus. Sandy speaks for them when she says, "There were all these things that the library could do for people that people had no idea [we] could do." She adds, "I think we need to let people know a little bit more what we have that could be useful to them," so in her unit she has "pulled together a new brochure. We send out blurbs about our new services to the departmental newsletters and just kind of basic stuff. We could do more."

Belief in "doing more" is a strong characteristic of this service ideal and parallels MOW IRT (1987) findings regarding workers who have strong service orientations. For example, Brenda and Fran speak for many librarians when the former frets that "we could spend more time with people who need it" and the latter sees "there are things we could do better" for users. Librarians will even bend some rules when that is the best way to serve users. Mark illustrates this in commenting that although users are not supposed to go into archival stack areas, "yesterday we violated that because we had a researcher who needed to see one thing from each year and each year was in a separate box." Karen sums up the essence of MIRI-U librarians' concept of service by saying, "I don't like the feeling that there's something I can't give [users]."

When asked What do you try to achieve as a librarian?, the librarians respond along three levels of increasingly abstract thought: personal gratification, positive effect on others, and symbolic idealization. Personal gratification is the most pragmatic level of response. Shelley illustrates this: "My [own] satisfaction, and that's one of the reasons I like my job so much. All the little things, [including] doing a good search for someone. [It's] when somebody finds something they didn't find the first time, and they come back the next day and thank us." Both Mike and Bob include "working for myself" as being very satisfying. Fran expresses some details of personal gratification when she talks of achieving as maintaining "balance . . . calm, [and] my head above water." Another view of this pragmatic conceptualization comes from Brenda, who says that achieving means "being very competent at what I do and having some influence on how things go." Margaret measures achievement in terms of completions: "[When I] beat my last year's statistics or get projects done on time," measuring success by whether she has "some fun while I'm doing it." For Elizabeth, becoming expert in specific areas is key to what she seeks to achieve as a librarian: to have "the kind of knowledge no one else will have." This sentiment is shared in part by Judith, who especially values "contribut[ing] to the life of the university . . . [and] making things happen in my own sphere." Mike sums up the idea of achievement as personal gratification. He believes achievement is met when he is prepared—sharing his knowledge with others, making his service "special" for everyone, and "giving 100 percent" in all interactions.

Representing a higher level of abstraction, MIRI-U librarians also see achievement in the positive effect their activities have on others, especially users. This type of achievement also fits MOW IRT's (1987) conceptions of service-oriented work and is part of the librarians' characterization of the profession of academic librarianship. Librarians divide interactions with users into finding things for them and making them independent so they can find their own things. This latter activity splits into teaching users about the library's resources and services, and increasing access points to resources.

In concert with most literature on assisting library users, MIRI-U librarians feel a strong sense of achievement when their work results in user independence (see, for example, selections on library instruction in *Information for a New Age* [ALA 1995]). Those doing reference work feel high personal gratification in resolving complex information needs and high professional success when increased numbers of users ask more articulated and complex questions rather than poorly phrased, basic ones. The significance of this aspect of a service ideal is seen in Lynne's belief that part of her teaching role lies in "encouraging people to understand why" as well as how. Librarians in open-stack locations in the library system place teaching independence at the high end and actually finding answers for users at the low end of a valuing scale. However, those in closed areas, especially archives, place "making any collection as easy to use as possible" (Elaine) at the front end of user independence and their own levels of satisfaction. In their case, this, by necessity, includes "providing access to the information that people need" (Mark).

Those who see providing access as the form of achievement generally have responsibility for aspects of the online catalog or they are involved with electronic technology—be that online searching, programming, or editing text or data. For Andy, providing access is making the catalog "better" each and every day so those using it increase their probability of finding what they are seeking. In the medical library, Patti sees it in "connecting" people to the information they need—through use of various tools and/or services. Several librarians speak of access as an "opening-up" activity. They frame it in terms of increasing the array of user search options or resources. Brooke talks of supporting reference librarians and users by "enhancing the record" of reference tools to include key words and contents, and of increasing cross-references in the online catalog. Michele envisions systems in her data archive "good enough [so users] can grab information, they can do it and they don't need you."

The third and most abstract conceptualization of achievement is symbolic. Some MIRI-U librarians try to make others on campus see the library as an independent strength, rather than as primarily a support service to academic units. Others strive to do "everything with a high degree of quality" (Margaret) or "to provide a service that has integrity" (Mary). At its broadest conception, achieving as a librarian is symbolic of "contributing to society" (Nancy). There is a sense among these individuals that in carrying out their work, they can and should influence what is set in a sphere larger than their own desk or unit. Tony expresses this sentiment when he talks of "building for the future more than the here-and-now, anticipat[ing] what future needs are going to be." Elaine reflects all three levels of achievement when she talks of making a user's "job as painless as possible and our job as painless as possible."

Exercising Choice

In addition to valuing their profession and achieving satisfaction in their work, MIRI-U librarians passionately embrace the ideal of exercising choice over work and over as much of work life as possible. Within the constraints of MIRI-U as an institution and the library as an organization, they seek autonomy, variety, fun, and scope for individual action. These values reflect common attitudes of professionals and illustrate a noninstrumental orientation toward work—as a value in itself rather than as a means to reach other goals (Freidson 1986; MOW IRT 1987; Trice 1993; Ruiz Quintanilla 1990).

Autonomy is equated with intellectual and personal freedom, and MIRI-U librarians feel strongly about it. Although the degree of autonomy librarians believe they have is associated in some measure with the library's structure and culture, it also varies with physical location, type of primary work, and each librarian's sense of her or his own degree of control and responsibility for work. In terms of location, Elaine runs an archive and speaks for most archivists, curators, and many subject librarians:

We're pretty autonomous. The library doesn't impose too many demands on us as such. There's basic things, like you have to do your annual report by thus-and-such a date, but other than that, they don't really have a great understanding of what we do so they let us alone.

Indeed, being separate is positively valued when autonomy goes along with it, but "when it doesn't, it's bad news" (Galen). As he explains, in the science library, "we're separate, but we don't have the autonomy or the power to act separately." In sharp contrast, Patti describes the medical library as one place where central library administrators have "historically left us alone more than other units [and] that's fine."

In terms of types of work, Elizabeth believes "it was the initiative and independence that a bibliographer has" that attracted her to MIRI-U's library. She particularly values being able to initiate activities, whether they are continuing tasks or discrete projects. Referring to her catalog work, Margaret illustrates the enjoyment librarians feel about their specialties: "The nice thing about being the only person who knows any[thing about my field] is that at least nobody can look over my shoulder and tell me what I did wrong. . . . They don't nitpick at you. They give you your job and let you pretty much do it." She adds that she is "really horrified" at the lack of autonomy she hears associated with various other universities. Essentially, MIRI-U librarians believe the library's structure is such that "you're given the flexibility" (Sandy) to do your work as you choose to do it. Patti believes:

there's a lot of autonomy. And I think you develop that after working here. I mean, if you were some sort of person who went off on these tangents—and we've had people like that— then they have to be brought in. But I think if you prove yourself, that what you work on has been useful, then they pretty much let you go, which is wonderful.

Judith revels in being able to structure her own day because it is "enormously freeing." She adds, "I'm very autonomous. I really like it a lot. There's really nobody looking over me telling me, Now you should do this, now you should do that. I am in charge of my own schedule.

. . . I can set my own priorities as to when and how I do what." MIRI-U librarians firmly believe they know what they need to do and are the best judges of how to arrange work to fit their own work styles. Sandy, who comes to academic librarianship from work as a scientific researcher, contrasts her current experience with previous nonlibrarian jobs:

> I was always doing somebody else's work. . . . I had some control of what I did, [but] I feel in this job a lot of it is my own work. And I feel like I have a lot more freedom to do things that are more interesting and creative. . . . Five years ago, I would have thought, Oh, well, that's self-centered or not productive. I wouldn't have thought that was a positive thing. But now that I'm doing [this work], I think of it as a really positive thing. And the end goal is for the users all the time, but I get to take my own track. . . . I never used to be someone who had problems with saying no until I took this job. . . . Now I do, and it's really fun.

As noted previously, librarians reflect typical professional attitudes when they include having control over work while talking about autonomy. And to have control means taking responsibility for activities—having authority over situations. For example, Galen illustrates what control means by contrasting it with reference desk work, "which is totally uncontrolled," and he sees turning to other tasks over which he exercises more control as a welcome "sort of antidote" for reference desk work. Librarians measure responsibility in terms of "[our] own standards" (Elizabeth), which suggests ownership over tasks. MIRI-U librarians are quite clear that being responsible for tasks is meaningless if they are not also involved in "some of the decision-making" related to it (Chris). Subject librarians use control and responsibility terms most frequently, in part because their span of authority is wider and includes more types of work than that of other librarians. However, even though a subject librarian, Peg expresses what MIRI-U librarians see in general as the true value of autonomy: "The great satisfaction [over the years] is that I never really stopped growing in the job. [I have] a job that I could make pretty much what I wanted to, do it as much as I wanted to."

Responsibility, autonomy, and satisfaction are also associated with having variety in their work. The librarians see variety as giving meaning to one's primary work: "Everything that you do is informed by the sense of what happens in the other segments of it" (Mark). MIRI-U librarians clearly believe they are "not nailed to one subject" (Elaine). Or, as Andy puts it: "I deal with everything. I like that." Having a mixture of associated tasks comprise one's work also enables librarians to learn "different things, and [that means] not doing exactly the same thing every day" (Margaret). As we saw in the discussion of primary work, variety is a common element in all types of librarian work. It is related to autonomy and choice in that librarians control aspects of each task making up their work. For example, Nancy writes in her journal about preferring a specific kind of weekend desk schedule. Margaret describes how she structures her workdays to include a range of activities from reading e-mail to cataloging to researching projects, noting that "I get to do a little bit of everything actually. . . . I have probably more variety than most people." In contrasting her work with that of catalogers, Sandy believes, "I have a lot more variety in my job than they do."

An intriguing thing about the way MIRI-U librarians envision their work is exemplified in Sandy's comment: ascribing to others a lack of variety—a negative work characteristic. This is especially the case between catalogers and noncatalogers. Sandy does reference work as her primary work. She credits herself with having more variety than "they do"—referring to catalogers. Yet Margaret, who is a cataloger, says the same thing, though from the opposite direction. One cataloger believes many librarians think reference workers have more variety because they see "people out in public services as being a little more excited about their jobs and enthusiastic" (Chris). This suggests that moving around from task to task and direct librarian-user interaction are easily typified as demonstrating variety. Because those activities are common to reference work, catalogers are presumed to have less variety because their work takes place from within a single physical location with less contact between librarians, colleagues, and users. Across the library system, librarians believe their own work contains variety—perhaps more than librarians doing other kinds of work. MIRI-U librarians would agree that the way to get most librarians to quit their jobs is to make them do only one thing "eight hours a day for forty-odd weeks" (Pat). The only difficulty is that what looks like work with little or no variety to one librarian may look like work with a lot of variety to another.

MIRI-U librarians who believe their activities contain a lot of variety also believe their work is fun. More than half the librarians use both words when describing "work." They identify as fun those tasks that are especially enjoyable or highly satisfying and see work-as-fun as a frequent job occurrence. To researchers, this is part of the noninstrumental, intrinsic approach to working that finds autonomy, a range of interesting activities related to primary work, and active involvement in one's job to be particularly meaningful (Freidson 1986, Ruiz Quintanilla 1990). To the librarians, work-as-fun signifies creative activity, containing elements of unexpected pleasure.

The particular things that librarians find fun vary among individuals. In talking about the value of reference work, Elaine finds that "the fun comes in when you get something that you've never been asked before and you have to start exploring a whole new line of thinking." Galen says it was "really gratifying" to write a script for mass online catalog training. He experiences similar enjoyment in developing a software program to help others in a unit whose work is very different from his own. And he feels unexpected pleasure in teaching new staff: "You find . . . that you know things they have to learn, things you have to teach." In commenting on "really neat" things going on in the library and the university, Lynne says, "It is really fun to be surrounded by so many people who are doing so many interesting things." This attitude extends into her own work, one part of which is getting to "play" with hard questions and old documents. Rose agrees, noting that "I have always put a high value on...playing around with something and seeing how to make it work."

Sandy exemplifies fairly new librarians, who tend to be excited by discoveries. She calls it "fun to be [in a particular subject library] that's a little bit on the experimental . . . [and] being able to sort of try [something] out and get to know about it, and not have to just read about it somewhere and hope you get to see it someday." However, it is not just librarians embarking on their careers who see fun in discovering things. Elaine, who has worked with archival material for more than a decade, still finds "there is always something to do. And often you're handling new material all the time. I mean, not in the sense of new necessarily, but different." In anticipating work on a new research topic, Judith explains that "I've never done this [kind of research] before. So it's fun to be doing it."

Receiving and working with new subject materials also are occasions for discovery: "It's really exciting...just opening the boxes, sorting the stuff we want to keep, tossing everything else. . . . [One was] really a rich addition to what we had. That was very exciting" (Tony). Part of what happens when librarians do exciting things is that they create something new, and that has great significance for them. Elizabeth talks about enjoying "the assembling of a body of information applied to a question" and of the intellectual fun in teaching a class "everything...I thought they needed to know about the organization of information and how to use that in their research." And in commenting on piloting a particular project, Brooke says there was great value in "doing that—just for fun, just to see how it went."

Were it not for the support provided by researchers such as Freidson (1986, 1994) and others who study professions and work, it would be tempting to say that librarians having fun are being frivolous with their work—not taking it seriously. That would be an erroneous conclusion. As is typical of professionals and those who have strong work ethics, MIRI-U librarians associate the most fun with those tasks that comprise their particular primary work. The simple satisfaction of being "in charge of my own thing and just being able to do my own thing" (Judith) is a basic part of the concept of fun. And although highly satisfying activities can involve working with others in something "so exciting, I just wanted to be involved in it" (Chris), Judith illustrates the basic point when she says, "I really enjoy the hands-on contact with books and with people who read the books, and sort of running [my job] myself; I really do enjoy that." In other words, when the tasks they were hired to do, and those that librarians create for themselves, mesh with their sense of achievement, autonomy, control, and variety, librarians simply describe their work life as "just great. It's really fun. That's good" (Lynne).

A common thread to these significance-carrying aspects of work is a pervasive desire to be actively involved with one's work. Whether through participation in secondary task "citizenship duty" (Mark) or their own primary work, librarians act. One characteristic of such action is that it involves personal initiative. Galen represents many librarians when he muses, "I don't know if I attract it or it attracts me, but somehow I always find these little things that need doing and get them done. . . . I mean, it's all there. You have to be involved in *all* of it" (emphasis his). Because they feel they act deliberatively in their own work, MIRI-U librarians have little interest or patience in having themselves or other librarians portrayed as passive. They exemplify Scherdin's (1994) findings that librarians are imaginative and decisive, and demonstrate leadership, rather than earlier stereotypes of librarians as meticulous and lacking in self-confidence (Douglass [1957] in Wilson [1982]). Indeed, passivity is not part of Elizabeth's vocabulary: "We are not servile; we are not subordinate." And Michele illustrates this kind of proactive stance by noting that part of being in a research library means you "stake out your end at the high end . . . and put your money where your mouth is. [You] get out there."

MIRI-U librarians tend regularly to look for what they can do next, play with, or experiment on. Within subject bibliography, Elizabeth "simply took [on a new field] because I thought we were doing badly at it." She is typical of many subject bibliographers who find themselves developing subject areas even, she says, "in the face of opposition from some of my patrons." Satisfaction comes later, when students begin working on topics related to that area, and new or revised courses spring up. Librarians send recommendations to faculty about materials they believe will enhance course content or offerings. They take courses or sit down on their own "to learn how to use computers and DOS and commands . . . [to] investigate directories and that sort of thing" (Fran). And when they believe their subject library or work is not well understood by nonlibrarians, they find time to push outreach. Although admitting she has little extra time, Sandy reflects this latter point when she says, "I'm just sort of doing it on the side when I'm not doing something else." In archival work, librarians regularly pursue material they believe will enhance existing collections or "that we think are going to be more valuable as time goes on" (Tony).

In library instruction, librarians routinely decide what to include in course presentations. Through contacts at reference desks, they identify weak research and writing skills of students—targeting courses and developing sessions to address deficiencies. Reference work itself is a matter of "asking the right questions . . . to get [a user] into the right direction [so] I can categorize the question and get it in the vicinity of the answer. . . . And then I [can] find the answer" (Nancy). Or, as Elaine suggests, "sometimes they kind of have to be led." Deliberate action also means suggesting to a user at a public terminal "five different ways you might go about that [search]" (Shelley).

MIRI-U librarians believe that complexity is inherent to libraries, so they tend to look for things that improve efficiency in their own services. They routinely undertake research and development of products such as Web pages, online indexes, and journal abbreviations and locators. They watch for things that users or colleagues might need in the future. Nancy learned online searching when she was in library school "because I knew that it was going to be important." It was not part of the curriculum, but that did not matter to her. Even now, she says, "I do not believe that the library world has taken to computers fast enough." In her subject library, Elaine values being "on top of things," adding that "we hear about things before they've happened" by being attuned to what materials users are asking for or using. And, in discussing catalog work, Chris notes the need "to start doing some research to find out what it is we should be doing as catalogers" in a rapidly changing electronic work world.

Several librarians act as change agents—seeing their work as shaping user knowledge. Elaine reflects this when she says, "Sometimes in doing this [particular] historical research, whether or not that person can actually do the project may really be affected by whether there are existing records or not. Or [by] whether we can find them—because if we can't find any source material, then they have to abandon that project." She also finds herself guiding what researchers know by choosing which related materials to bring to their attention. Judith believes librarians frequently serve as change agents but adds that many "don't look at [them]selves in that way," although Mark is clear that in his subject library he does filter what users see "on the basis of sort of perceived need to know." Active involvement ranges from descriptively interpreting an item to create the image it will have in MIRIUCAT to controlling access to collections to "doing cross-fertilization" (Michele) between the library and various state agencies. Ultimately, users arrive at new knowledge through their own creative work. But librarians do serve as change agents and shapers of knowledge because as Judith sagely suggests:

> It's very much how . . . and what you present to [users that] influences what sort of information they find. . . . Although

> I think a librarian's role is traditionally one of intermediary and facilitator, [plus] gathering information and helping people find it, . . . we should realize that *how* we do those things does have an impact on *what* people do (emphasis hers).

Librarians believe most of the decision-making aspects of their work require independent judgment calls, which is typical of highly involved professionals (Freidson 1986; Abbott 1988). This sense of authority is seen when Margaret talks of reaching a point in one project where she finally said, "OK, we're not going to input any more garbage records." Or, as Tony phrases it: "Mine is the last word on all of the collections I have under my direction." Authority combines with practicality in many of the experiments and decisions librarians undertake. Galen develops an online program for another unit—working ideas back and forth until it performs in a way that is "very satisfying to see." Another librarian tends to reject developing grant proposals in favor of plans that can be accomplished with current resources and some ingenuity. A third one allows for that "sudden something else that pops up" unexpectedly to alter a proposal (Karen). However, there are personal attributes of MIRI-U librarians that flavor these deliberate actions. Some librarians are simply competitive; others strive to retain flexibility in approaching any and all tasks. And, Nancy suggests, many "fit in around average probably . . . [where] it just feels comfortable." Getting caught up in their work, librarians find themselves driven by their own standards. "I always want to be striving. . . . I like making things happen," says Judith. In certain areas, librarians do indeed have "some very firm opinions" (Tony) and push forward those activities they see as valuable to users, to themselves, or to the library system. They feel in a position to say "I know just what to do" (Sandy)— then, they go do it.

Given such active work lives and committed professional values, it is not surprising that the librarians have mixed emotions when asked how they assess their current positions in the library. Responses come like this one from Judith: "I am swamped! . . . generally happy to come to work in the morning and wondering very much what it is that I will do next." Those who agree with the "swamped" part tend to see themselves as reluctant beneficiaries of staff cuts during periods when technology and increased enrollments require more time with each user interaction. Or, as

Fran phrases it, "[I am] stretched past the maximum. . . . I am learning new things every day [that] make changes affecting the way services are provided." These librarians consider their specific mixture and variety of tasks as both challenging and frustrating. Disappointment is expressed in terms of lack of recognition, reward, encouragement, or appreciation for work well done. Success is found in keeping one's head above water.

Those who focus on the "happy" part have a variety of reasons for that feeling. Some point to maintaining a balance between their work and home lives. Others would agree with Andy, who stresses the autonomous nature of his work: "I am free to do a lot of decision-making on how I spend my time. . . . I can sort of choose what I want to do and feel like I'm contributing in whichever way I think is the best for that moment." Several subject librarians delight in having a lot of variety in their work. Karen represents them when she says she enjoys being "a wearer of many hats." In addition, all these librarians have close colleagues with whom they work.

Some MIRI-U librarians think first in position description terms, and then add that they like helping others learn about and understand specific job-related tasks. These librarians focus on the specialized nature of their work. A few find themselves "not entirely satisfied" (Chris), feeling their strengths and abilities are not yet fully tapped. Chris adds that she'd like to see more excitement in both her own work and the library system as a whole. Overall, and in their various ways, MIRI-U librarians reflect what Mark says: "I am fulfilled, important, useful; I am able to help other people. That sounds trite, [but] I *am* able to match people's needs with available resources."

I Have the Ideal Job

A strong majority of MIRI-U librarians believe they have the ideal job for their interests and needs. As noted earlier in this chapter, they stay in the field because they like the "fit." Factors supporting this perception include the close similarity between a typical and an ideal day, the thinkwork involved in doing primary work and, for some of the librarians, the opportunity to purse scholarship.

For MIRI-U librarians, a typical day contains tasks mostly associated with primary work. Generally, librarians set their own schedules based on activities over which they have control and on meeting arrangements. Andy illustrates this combination: "I have meetings that get scheduled, but other than that, I can pretty much decide *when* I want to do *what* I want to do" (emphasis his). Elizabeth, a subject bibliographer, outlines her typical day: "[It] varies . . . depending on meetings that I may have, or a course that may meet, or the students who come to me. And it varies from the early to the late part of the term. The constants in my day are [going through] selection tools so I can keep up with the book trade." For librarians engaged in reference work, a typical day revolves around a reference desk schedule or, in Michele's case, "processing new incoming data, setting up files, and just trying to get all the bureaucratic things shuffled and done and out of the way."

MIRI-U librarians agree that typical and ideal workdays contain variety and achievement. The following represents a range of expressions regarding what they believe makes for an ideal day:

> Galen [does primarily reference work]: I really like the public contact on a pretty regular basis at the reference desk. So I think an ideal day would include some of that, it would include programming, and [going for] a good run on a spring day. . . . I think an ideal day would have no meetings.

> Tony [archivist]: [It is] one when I've lined up a donor for a collection that perhaps we've been after for years. . . . That sense of accomplishment of wrapping up some things that have been going on for a long time, getting some big project done. . . . It's also a nice feeling on days when I don't have a damned thing to do . . . catch up on reading . . . opening the boxes [of a new collection].

> Lynne [subject library unit head]: [It's] having some wonderful brand-new documents come in and say, "Wow! That's really cool". . . . A particularly good day is when you're at the desk and some really neat people come and use stuff, and you get to play [with] the kind of hard questions that have to do with old documents. . . . Then you find [what someone needs] and they say, "Oh, that's just marvelous! It's just ex-

actly what I want. How in the world did you do that?". . . . And it's a good day when your staff gets something really good done and feels pleased about it.

Brooke [cataloger]: As much as I enjoy the company of other people, if I could just have it quiet and listen to the radio and do what work I wanted to without the phone ringing, or what work I needed to do without the phone ringing and without people carrying on about this, that, or the other. . . . Once a week would be good. Twice a week, that would be past heaven!

Across MIRI-U's library system, both typical and ideal workdays are filled with "thinkwork" (Hales 1980). That term, which identifies intellectual activity that includes problem-solving, reflects what MIRI-U librarians strongly prefer to see in their work. Such thinking ranges from very detailed, narrow, focused levels (e.g., explaining how to find a title in MIRIUCAT) to very abstract, highly creative levels (e.g., rule interpretation or creating a smooth transition between a user's original question and his or her actual need). It also incorporates the type of research that leads to published communication of new knowledge.

Practical problem-solving is routine in much daily work. Andy illustrates this when he describes a typical day as one where "I pick up a problem I've been working on in the database or a problem that's been left or is given to me . . . by one of my staff or one of the other librarians." And as with most work, "there is the perfect satisfaction of getting the little problems resolved because bigger problems . . . go on and on and on" (Karen). However, not all thinking is linear. Michele finds that with many tasks "you start off here, and you bop off there, and that brings an idea out here, and you go back there . . . ." This more abstract, unpredictable thinking level is readily apparent in reference work, where Brenda sees resolving users' questions as "figur[ing] out (a) what they're saying and (b) what they want. And then trying to gear your response to the level that they're on. And trying to determine what they're going to understand and what's going to be too complicated." Or, as Mark sees it, "are [they] really ready to move into something else without knowing it." In catalog work, librarians engage in such abstract thinkwork when they move beyond "formulas and titles and authors and key words" (Mark) into rule interpretation and questions of system design.

Yet another level of thinkwork is envisioning both parts and wholes—especially patterns to parts that make up wholes. Librarians doing archival tasks frequently engage in this kind of thinking, such as when Mark talks of "the archives [as] like an onion or something. There are so many things within concentric circles or layers of the onion." Viewing one's tasks as an organic whole is also descriptive of collection work where, throughout their subject areas, librarians seek to balance today's requirements for specific materials with anticipated future needs. For many MIRI-U librarians, seeing both parts and wholes is a natural function of "the work I do, as an intellectual process" (Michele). They consider it an act of bringing things to a higher level of generality, whether a set of tasks or a single activity. In general, the librarians like "to build worlds. . . . I like to make things happen" (Judith). It is "the satisfaction in seeing the totality—the machine working with all the little parts twittering and moving and spinning, all run[ning] smoothly in detail," says Andy.

For some MIRI-U librarians, that "totality" comes into view only through conducting research and publishing the results. This activity is carried out either as means to an end when related to primary work or as a goal itself. For untenured librarians, the initial impetus for publishing activity comes from the need to build a dossier for consideration of continuing appointment. Karen, for instance, is "working on a project in order to get a paper published." Yet, it is clear that she also enjoys the research aspect on its own merit because she wants "to publish an article on a topic that hasn't been done before—to feel like I'm [doing] something worthwhile." Yet, as part of primary work, this form of thinkwork evidences itself mostly in user-oriented publications and in identifying and analyzing library materials and services. Chris illustrates task relationship by explaining that "part of cataloging involves doing research. And we use the research collections here as well as catalog them." Judith, a subject bibliographer, echoes this, noting that "actually being able to get into these resources is just great." Sometimes what starts as a local, task-related activity develops into a larger enterprise, as when Margaret wrote "a little position paper on some cataloging questions [related to] a survey" and sent it to the surveyor, who "called and asked if they could establish a position of visiting associate, would I come and help her for from three to six months." Mary is typical of those with a task focus when she says she likes being involved in research activities, but "if I'm going to do research . . . I want it to be in the service of something that's going to make a difference."

There is a group of MIRI-U librarians who see time as their major research constraint. Peg finds that "I have had a fair amount of stress trying to do all of these other things, which have spilled into the time that I use to do research." And Bob grumbles that regular involvement in too many things means "what you don't have [here] is actually enough time to spend on any research that you might be doing." Michele longs to "take six months off and take a laptop computer and a big battery pack, and head off . . . [to] think and write. . . . See, to me [lack of time is] a really frustrating thing . . . because it's through writing that you 'connect' with other people."

Peg, Bob, Michele, and the untenured Karen are among those MIRI-U librarians who see research and publication as goals in themselves and integral to work life. They are openly enthusiastic about this kind of thinkwork, and each one has "a deep feeling for the research process" (Rose). Peg says, "I have been asked, Do you think of yourself as a librarian or a scholar? I don't separate [them]." Regardless of their primary work, this group feels that research is a normal part of work, and "you don't feel that you [are] a good librarian without doing it" (Karen). All the tenured members of this group have completed numerous articles and monographs. Their future research efforts include a number of projects. Bob plans a sourcebook characterizing "the fathers and the mothers" of a specific discipline. Michele wants to take a theoretical look at "the implications of the technological revolution in the creation, dissemination, and access to information [in terms of] who are the winners, who are the losers, and how do you get things done." Rose is "interested in doing a hypertext publication [on a particular author] and maybe putting it out there on the Net." Other thinkwork scholars include Tony and Nancy. The former is developing a collaborative study of "firms using [specific online] systems [to] get some hard data on what kind of information is being lost," whereas Nancy is considering reducing her contractual work hours in order to have more time for scholarship. Elizabeth speaks for all when she says, "I'm sort of discombobulated . . . when I'm not writing or working on any piece of research." And the idea of not doing research is foreign to Peg. Although she does not want to become "just a researcher," when she thinks about retiring she believes "I certainly would continue to do research; in fact, there are about three projects I'm putting off. . . . [Work and scholarship] is how I divide up my life."

Conclusion

Reflecting numerous studies on different types of work, Kohn (1990, 43) concludes that "job conditions not only affect, but also are affected by, personality," and Roberson (1990, 107) finds that individuals' "work meanings influence work motivation and performance." This chapter has shown that the MIRI-U librarians verify such assertions. The significance they give specific concepts meld with their ideas about primary work and their work setting to round out a psychological and organizational sense of self and an overall sense of work identity. It is clear that MIRI-U librarians value being academic librarians. It bestows upon them a professional identity associated with learning, teaching, and scholarship. They take responsibility for independently made decisions and view their work as being important for themselves and for users. Confirming Freidson (1986) and Ruiz Quintanilla (1990), the librarians express intrinsic motivation that values work for its own sake as well as for what it might bring in instrumental rewards. Put in MOW IRT (1987) terms, they see this work as central to their life experiences.

They are relatively forgiving of users who do not know a librarian from a student assistant. However, they prefer for professional colleagues individuals who approach library tasks as thinkwork and puzzle-solving. Likewise, the librarians are partial to users who combine independent learning with help from librarians to master new information and knowledge-seeking techniques and resources. A service ideal operates when the librarians give order, on behalf of users, to the chaos inherent in the random information found in library materials while—at the same time—enabling users to make order out of the chaos inherent in the latter's own unarticulated needs. Achievement at the gratification, effect, or symbolic level is a result of accomplishing things for themselves and for library users.

These librarians see meaningfulness in their work, believe they experience responsibility for outcomes of that work, and generally feel they know the actual results of their work activities. According to Hackman and Oldham (1980), these are crucial psychological states that must exist if one is to (1) feel internally motivated to do one's work and (2) be satisfied with the results. The core characteristics that must exist for these states to develop are skill variety, task identity, task significance, autonomy, and feedback from the work itself (Hackman and Oldham 1980). The first three characteristics reflect meaningfulness. *Skill variety* is an obvious part of the librarians' lives at work. They are constantly drawing on a number of different personal skills and talents, along with the inherent variety of tasks associated with their work. *Task identify* refers to doing a job from beginning to end with a visible outcome. Primary work is seen as such an intact activity by each librarian, even though it must be combined with secondary tasks and other work to fulfill a librarywide mission. Hackman and Oldham (1980, 79) define the third core characteristic related to meaningfulness, *task significance*, as "the degree to which the job has a substantial impact on the lives of other people, whether those people are in the immediate organization or in the world at large." Regardless of their particular tasks, MIRI-U librarians believe that what they do influences what users find and how users think about what they have found. This is also reflected in the librarians' expression of effect and symbolic achievement.

Autonomy is the core job characteristic that Hackman and Oldham believe allows one to experience responsibility for work outcomes. Library work is thinkwork that requires autonomy because much of it rests on constant, complex, individual judgment. Diagnosing immediate needs, pondering future needs, and creating information representation and order all take creative thinking. Indeed, Asher (1995, 72) argues that "on-the-job autonomy is the single most important predictor of people's degree of satisfaction with their work," and Freidson (1986, 141) avers that it is "the minimal characteristic of the professional employee." Intimately coupled with autonomy is control, and MIRI-U librarians believe they are most creative and do highest-quality work when they control the various tasks that comprise work. The notion of control also illustrates Hackman and Oldham's (1980, 80) final core characteristic: feedback from the work itself. Librarians feel they know the actual results of their work activities because carrying out their primary work provides them with "direct and clear information about the effectiveness of [their] performance." At MIRI-U, this is expressed in most of the concepts discussed in this and the preceding two chapters. Finally, those who feel they have autonomy, control, variety, and choice in their work life also believe their work is fun to do. Part of making work fun is conscious, active involvement in choosing what and when to do the set of tasks that constitutes especially their primary work. When all these significance-meaning elements come together for a librarian, the fit is good, and he or she is most likely to say, "I have the ideal job."

5. A Postindustrial Future

There is national consensus among those who study the sociology and psychology of work that places of work, work itself, and perceptions of work are changing. In very fundamental ways, work is becoming increasingly complex, and the balance in carrying it out "has tipped from hand to head, from brawn to brain. Workers don't just run machines and push paper; they control information" (Howard 1995b, 23). These changes have led researchers to promote the idea of a postindustrial workforce and society. For example, Hage and Powers (1992, 13) believe that professional, managerial, and technical workers will become the new majority, there will be many more occupational specialties than before, and tasks will be able to be combined in so many different ways that it will become increasingly difficult to speak of a "typical" position. They identify nine role dimensions across which the nature of work can be contrasted (see figure 1). The work and work lives of MIRI-U librarians illustrate many of the ideal-type characteristics of a postindustrial organization.

For the adhocratic, academic world, mental activity is already the norm. Higher education rests on information-gathering and problem-solving activities. Particularly within the research university, disciplinary faculty and librarians expect to have high levels of autonomy and strong involvement in decision-making. Expanding knowledge within and outside campus borders has converted generalists to specialists, and even though librarians, faculty, and other campus professionals may have vari-

Figure 1. The Contrast between the Nature of Work in Industrial and Postindustrial Society.

Ideal-Type Characteristics of Industrial Roles	Ideal-Type Characteristics of Postindustrial Roles
1. Physical activity.	1. Mental activity.
2. Transformation of material objects (e.g., picking fruit, smelting iron, assembling toasters, ironing clothes, transporting plywood, selling shoes).	2. Information-gathering and problem-solving.
3. Roles defined in terms of a narrow range of prescribed tasks and routine activities for which goals and procedures are clearly specified.	3. Roles defined by goals for which no certain procedure can be specified, consequently involving a relatively wide range of nonroutine tasks.
4. Time and place for role performance tightly constrained and there is freedom from role-related concerns when outside that place in time and space.	4. The time and place for role activity are not tightly constrained, and people have difficulty insulating one social domain (e.g., family or work) from worries or demands emanating from other domains.
5. Humans as appendages of machines: machines determine how the work is to be done, how long it will take, and what the finished product will look like.	5. People determine how work will be done, how much time will be spent, and what the finished product will look like; machines are tools.
6. Satisfactory job performance produces a sense of completion.	6. Satisfactory job performance a sense of mastery.
7. Nonephemeral aspects of roles resist change.	7. Roles are frequently and substantially redefined via negotiations and even conflict.
8. Low interaction rates, even for managers; that is, the role set is small and contained.	8. High interaction rates; that is, the role set is large and demanding.
9. Service is a small component of most jobs.	9. Service is a significant component of many roles.

able contract requirements, it is common for all of them to independently decide where, when, and how to carry out their responsibilities. Discord may occur if job performance is defined as productivity rather than achievement (Bolman and Deal 1997). In academe, much of the first three-quarters of the twentieth century was spent defining the nature of one's work and establishing the right to control it; role prerogatives are jealously guarded (Rudolph 1962; Veysey 1965; Finkelstein 1984). At the end of the century, even with constrained budgets, variable enrollments, and increased calls for academic accountability to external constituents, the hallmarks of the research university are still those of "cultivating challenging education for highly talented undergraduates, providing the strongest graduate training in the world, performing research at the frontiers of knowledge, and sustaining a reservoir of expertise that can be called upon by American society" (Geiger 1993, 83). Such an environment does not necessarily welcome nor respond quickly to any kind of change.

However, in the mid-1990s, MIRI-U librarians find themselves in the midst of waves of alterations. Large-scale societal and technological pressures are becoming internalized on campus and across the library system. Whether responding to the collection and reference needs of a more diverse student body, answering e-mail from half the world away, or rethinking the balance between work and family roles, the librarians reflect postindustrial concerns as well as postindustrial ways of thinking. As noted in chapter 3, within the library system they are rethinking the organization's structure. The combination of organizational and societal changes will unfreeze existing practices and behavior patterns, encourage experimentation with new practices, and result in development of new standards and shared meanings and values. Will the new meanings and values inspired by internal and external changes be similar to, or fundamentally different from, those the librarians currently hold? An answer may be found by comparing what has been learned thus far with some basic conceptions about work and work centrality.

The Nature of Work
It is well to remember that an individual's life at work consists of content and context. Elements in the content realm include the physical and mental demands of each task; level of responsibility; scope for initiative and dis-

cretion; amount of variety; length of work cycle; level of skill; knowledge and experience required; degree of interaction with people; ideas and material objects called up; and scope for learning. Principal aspects of context are physical working conditions; safety and hazards to physical and mental health; length and arrangement of hours for work; security of tenure of one's existing job within the organization; pay and methods of payment; opportunities for advancement; fringe benefits; welfare services; coworkers; and status in the organization (OECD 1977). Each realm affects how MIRI-U librarians conceptualize their work and, ultimately, their work identity.

Work content encompasses tasks and associated demands and tools that specify those activities that, collectively, a librarian calls "my work." As a group, the librarians engage in collection, catalog, reference, and learning-teaching-training work. Each librarian defines her or his work as "primarily" one of the first three types.

Librarians begin building their work construct by choosing terms commonly found in generic position descriptions used within the library system. Onto that basic platform, each adds distinguishing characteristics that separate "my work" from that of other librarians in the same unit or library area. Thus, although a number of librarians might agree they all do collection work, each adds tasks that are solely her or his own or that extend beyond that platform to give the set of tasks a personalized character. In so doing, librarians develop a basic work identity (Strauss in Braude 1983). They define or name themselves in primary work terms—I am a reference librarian, I am a subject bibliographer—followed by specifics that allow each to set herself or himself apart from other reference librarians or subject bibliographers.

Many MIRI-U librarians would stop at this point, satisfied that this construct of primary work reflects their work. However, further analysis reveals various secondary tasks that effectively expand their notion of academic library work. For collection librarians, these activities cluster around individualized reference work in support of faculty and students from fields associated with the librarians' subject areas. Catalogers may include reference desk involvement, and reference librarians may add programming specialties to their unit's array of responsibilities. Librarians with the most integrated primary and secondary activities are found in subject libraries, where the scope of individual responsibility, span of control, and diversity of task are broader than in other library system units.

Finally, all the librarians engage at various times in tertiary activities: MIRI-U library projects, committee assignments, and service activities. Over half are involved in associations or organizations related to librarianship or their primary work. Most frequently, involvement is as a member or officer of one or more of these professional bodies: the American Library Association (especially its Association of College & Research Libraries division), the state library association, the Special Libraries Association, and specialist groups such as the Society for the History of Discoveries or the Society of American Archivists. MIRI-U librarians use these activities to further develop their specializations. For example, a cataloger works closely with RLG. A reference librarian attends conferences to ferret out new touch-screen products. A bibliographer serves on a committee developing new standards for evaluating collections. An archivist presents a paper on aspects of appraisal. At the state level, librarians share a general sense that as a research university "we're kind of looked upon . . . as the ones that are supposed to do things first and supposed to know about things a little bit more" (Sandy). Clearly, however, the librarians identify themselves in terms of primary work. It is the work content construct that most closely reflects those activities upon which librarians spend the greatest amount of time, by which they define themselves, and through which they gain a grounded psychological and sociological sense of self.

In a conceptual sense, MIRI-U librarians see work in abstract terms—as an idea given form by sharing meanings and experiences with each other. They develop that abstraction into "my work" by giving specific meaning to each task, activity, and experience for which they are individually responsible. Their concept of primary work governs how librarians think, how they give order to each day, the roles they assign to other librarians and nonlibrarians in their work world, the size of that work world, and their sense of place and fit within a life-at-work. Because the concept of primary work forms the core of their sense of work and self, librarians relate other meaningful aspects of their work and work lives to it: the closer the association, the stronger the significance. They understand, take part in, and extend their definition of self to other aspects of work life in terms of the influence they believe such aspects exert on their primary work.

To give an example, consider a set of concentric circles. MIRI-U librarians would place primary work in the innermost one. One circle away would come colleagues, regardless of unit affiliation or type of work—although those doing the same or similar primary work have the strongest connections. Beyond collegiality is a circle that could be labeled "internal relations. Here, librarians place a mixture of MIRI-U library system-related matters. Some are structural, such as policy and management issues; others are more abstract, including issues of communication, loyalty, and responsibility. At this internal relations level, librarians become more selective about what to consider important. They begin to lose a complete view of, and understanding and involvement in, the larger work world. An even slightly more distant circle contains the remaining aspects of the library system as an organization. Significant matters are few and tend to be only those with connections to the carrying out of primary work or to responsibilities a librarian associates with being a member of a profession or status group. For most MIRI-U librarians, their interests stop at either the internal relationships arm or the organizational circles.

The outermost circle is MIRI-U as an institution. Few of the librarians are involved with it other than as general members of a university community. As a university and as an institution, MIRI-U has significant meaning for librarians in two sharply contrasting ways. It affects them personally in terms of funding and culture. It affects them in a more abstract fashion as a place of intellectual and research renown. The librarians know little about MIRI-U as a holistic entity. If given a choice, they would place themselves within the innermost circle in order to see their primary work most clearly. By the time MIRI-U is located on the farthest circle, the librarians would be able to see only a few images distinctly enough to identify them.

According to Ford (1975), Vander Zanden (1987), and other philosophers and social psychologists, knowing what a person values and prefers assists in giving shape to that individual. As bearers of meaning, values add definition to the librarians' work and work life constructs; preferences then provide a scale for those values. MIRI-U librarians clearly bestow great value, and positive preference, on primary work and the activities and situations they connect with that work. Even when experiencing frustration or difficulty with work-related matters, the librarians discuss and portray their work in very laudatory terms. Along with primary work, they vest colleagues with high, positive valuation. Those aspects of work and work life within the internal relationships circle carry both kinds of preferences. Service, achievement, and elements of choice have high, positive values. The library system as an organization and structure is within this level, and the librarians generally conceive of it as a positive value. However, they express neutral to negative preferences regarding many aspects of it. The more librarians perceive the organization as constraining those things they most value, the lower the value they accord the organization and the less preference they express for association with it. Looking at the outermost circle, librarians assign value to MIRI-U with positive preference to it as a university and negative preference for it as an institution.

Although the librarians separate valuing something from whether they prefer to have much interaction with it, they express both values and preferences in accord with Epstein's (1989) rational conceptual system. That is, they use conventional words, symbols, and rules of logic to convey meanings and give straightforward assessments of beliefs. However, they come close to Epstein's more affective, experiential conceptual system when reflecting on primary work. Meanings and values associated with primary work seem to be bending with work and societal changes more than being fundamentally altered by them.

Most of those who study the meaning work has for people believe that the influx of electronic technologies is behind fundamental changes in work and how it is perceived. Are the core meanings and values of MIRI-U librarians vulnerable to fundamental alteration in this regard? At the moment, the answer is no. During the 1960s through the 1980s, catalogers moved from local fine-tuning of Library of Congress records to contributing to national online databases (Hafter 1986). Reference librarians struggled with learning various online database-searching languages and catalog protocols. And as the 1990s began, collection librarians selected materials in an ever-widening array of print and nonprint, paper and electronic formats. Yet, by the mid-1990s, MIRI-U librarians essentially had absorbed electronic technologies into their value systems. They are clearly no longer in awe—seeing such technologies, instead, as tools for supporting traditional mediating and enabling roles. That is, the librarians see this technology not as creating a new type of work, but, rather, as another means to the same end: carrying out a service ideal of productively bringing user and information together.

Academic librarians now set high standards for electronic tools. As is characteristic of thinkworkers and problem solvers, they prefer pushing a piece of software to its limits rather than merely accepting what a manual says it can do. MIRI-U librarians research, develop, program, and modify computer products. They study the effects of various technologies on scholarly communication and on library material formats and use. Given their fundamental commitment to bringing order to information chaos, they feel particularly frustrated about the lack of consistency in standards and protocols. An example comes from Fran. Over the course of one recent year, her subject library received more than fifty separate compact disk titles, plus several CD-ROM subscription titles. She illustrates the sense of frustration, along with the concepts of service and proactive behavior, in her description of the problems associated with linking users with this technology:

> We try to . . . get [each online product] set up so a patron does not need to do anything but hit a couple of keys to start it running. [I work] through any documentation that comes with a CD-ROM to see if it reads well enough for what we consider the computer expertise of the patrons, [often] re-writing or writing something that will go step-by-step. For those disks with their own search software, we need to make our staff familiar enough with them so that they know when it might be appropriate to suggest [the tool] to a user. . . . With any disk, it may take five or six hours all together [before presenting it to users].

Brooke thinks that "as more and more people are doing their own searching, . . . the people on the reference desk have to be out there—to help people do [that] searching." That assistance is needed because, as Kong and Goodfellow (1988, 207) report, "consumers must now learn to cope with two major obstacles—information overload and information complexity."

Retaining their organizational skepticism, however, the librarians express concern that library- and university-level administrators do not yet fully grasp that changing from print to electronic tools means more, rather than less, librarian involvement. They fear there is, or could be, a push from administrators to reduce staffing levels because of availability of electronic resources. Brenda illustrates this concern:

> I think the feeling they [i.e., administrators] have is, Well, we have all these electronic sources, so we don't need as much mediation. But what we find is the more electronic sources we get, the more mediation is needed for the user. Because they're not familiar—, they're really not familiar with the databases on compact disk. Or even if they are, because there's not standardization, they need a lot of help.

In comparing electronic-based versus paper-based work, Sandy notes that "explaining how to use [online tools] is the part that's different than print [tools]. . . . It takes so much longer, and you can't just wander off on people as quickly when you're helping them. . . . They want you to sit there through their whole first couple of [searches] to see how they're doing." MIRI-U librarians also find an increasing number of users who, having developed their own home-based searching programs, telephone the reference desk to ask librarians "to revise [those] programs [over the phone] when things don't work" (Galen).

As is clear from their assignment of positive significance to the concepts of variety and fun, librarians prefer working with complex situations, and electronic tools are no exception. When they describe changes in their work and work lives, these librarians stress that technology-based change is not only positive, but also "is by far and away the biggest change" (Brooke). Yet it seems to have taken only ten years or so for online technologies to have simply become "part of the picture" for MIRI-U librarians (Galen).

In his *Wealth of Nations*, Adam Smith (1776) discussed five aspects of work that affect general employment. They are also relevant to individuals' perceptions of their own work:

1. The degree to which the work is agreeable or disagreeable to do;

2. The ease or difficulty, and the cheapness or expensiveness, of learning the work;

3. The constancy of employment;

4. The large or small amount of trust placed in the worker by others;
5. The probability or improbability of success in their work.

These concerns have remained basically unchanged as Western societies have moved from preindustrial through industrial and into late twentieth-century postindustrial frames of thinking and working. The meanings and values MIRI-U librarians express about their work illustrate all five aspects. The librarians have divided their work into primary and secondary clusters that reflect personal preferences and competencies, clearly favoring the former while not entirely rejecting the latter. They strongly believe their primary work is complex and challenging, and that it requires time-consuming, continuous learning. Although they may disagree with each other over particular employment statuses, rights, and responsibilities, it is difficult for them to conceive of working in any place other than an academic library. And, indeed, even when acknowledging workplace stresses, the librarians make no plans to terminate that employment. Both trust and success are highly prized and are seen as secured through gains made in autonomy, personal responsibility, recognition by one's peers, job satisfaction, and other elements contributing to the sense of having an ideal job.

Over the course of the twentieth century, academic librarians' work-related techniques have shifted from manual to electronic, and their knowledge base has evolved from technical competence to interpretative expertise. But this study of the MIRI-U librarians suggests that basic values and meanings associated with academic library work have been maintained. Across their library system, they still carry out Abbott's (1988, 40) "acts of professional practice": diagnosis, inference, and treatment. They still illustrate Merton's (1982) triad of professional values: knowing, doing, and helping. That is, they continually subject information to their own professional knowledge system, identify appropriate options for interpreting it, and convey it to others via collection, catalog, reference, and learning-teaching-training work. Although the means for doing their work may have changed, the raison d'etre is still to support the institutional mission by serving the needs of its members.

Work Centrality
The shape and focus that each librarian gives to her or his own work is

influenced by both the particular tasks comprising the work and the organization within which the work is done. To this truism, Ruiz Quintanilla and Wilpert (1988) add that how central working is to an individual can be viewed in two complementary, but essential, ways: centrality of work in relation to self and centrality of work in relation to other life roles. The former perspective sees work as playing either a major, a contributing, or a peripheral role in the construction of one's overall self-image. This "cognitive consistency process" approach is advanced by researchers such as Lodahl and Kejner (1965) and Lawler and Hall (1970). The view of the relative preference for work in comparison with various other life spheres is most notably associated with Dubin (1956). His "central life interests" approach compares each individual's preference for work activities with preferences for leisure, family, community, and other life roles.

For professionals such as academic librarians, one's training, ideological commitments, and service orientation also influence the particular meaning and centrality of work (Braude 1983). An early study using Dubin's approach compared nurses with industrial workers (Orzack 1959). Only in the areas of information relations and technological relations did the two groups score the same: Both groups experienced closer informal relations outside their work, and both experienced more technological relations at work. Otherwise, only the nurses saw their work as being the major focal point in their lives, as well as to their sense of personal satisfaction, and only they saw the workplace as their most meaningful formal organizational structure. This corresponds to the Friedmann and Havighurst (1954) study of retirees noted in chapter 1. Recall that they, also, found that only members of the sole professional group placed high value on service to others and considered their work to be a strongly positive aspect of their lives.

The centrality that work has for MIRI-U librarians can be found by comparing the meaning that working has for them with the Meaning Of Working (MOW) patterns England and Whitely (1990) developed from a subset of the original MOW International Research Team data. The framework England and Whitely used in their study rests on three MOW IRT components: work centrality, work goal preferences, and societal norms about working. The concept of *work centrality* parallels Dubin and is defined as "the degree of general importance that working has in the life of an individual at any given point in time" (England and Whitely 1990,

68). This phrase speaks to an identification with work, involvement, and commitment to work, and choosing working as a major mode of self-expression. *Work goal preferences* includes variety, autonomy, responsibility, pay, and a good match between an individual's job skill requirements and his or her abilities and experience. Goals are seen as incentives to work and as factors that may lead to the choice of one type of work over another. *Societal norms about working* focuses on entitlement and obligation. Both incorporate notions of justice: the right to rewards or opportunities, or duty and belief in contributing to society (MOW IRT 1987). Entitlement presupposes underlying rights of individuals and the work-related responsibility of society and organizations toward individuals. Obligation presupposes the underlying duties of individuals to their organization and to society. England and Whitely enhanced the centrality-preference-norms framework with demographic, work, and outcome variables. The demographic factors are age, gender, and educational level. Work is measured in terms of work goals, occupation position level, role within the individual's organization, length of the work week, and net monthly pay. Finally, the outcome variable is expressed as occupational satisfaction, commitment to work, and essential work values.

Eight work patterns (or categories) emerge from this enhanced framework, with each named so as to reflect its basic characteristics.[1] The meanings and values that MIRI-U librarians have expressed in this book fit most clearly into the Duty-Oriented Social Contribution Workers category. Both MOW IRT study participants in this category and MIRI-U librarians are employed in high-quality jobs characterized by wide variety, high autonomy, above average levels of responsibility, and high skill utilization. The majority of members of both groups are over thirty years old, and there is an overrepresentation of women. As members of a professional group, MIRI-U librarians have a particular higher education requirement; however, a college or university degree is a general characteristic of the duty-oriented individual. Managerial or supervisory responsibilities are typically held. And although they expect a fair salary, in concert with the MOW group, the librarians consider pay issues to be of generally less value than other aspects of work. Among the MIRI-U librarians, approximately half responded positively to the classic commitment question of whether they would leave librarianship if financially able to do so. Even then, for the librarians, figures ranged from $500,000 upward before economic values became more important than work-fit and work-identity associations.

A duty-oriented view is also expressed as MIRI-U librarians connect their concept of work with service to society. Some reflect this category in their high level of occupational and primary work satisfaction, others in their views on achievement. The librarians fit the category in their belief that if they could choose a career again, it would still be academic librarianship. It is likely a majority would agree with the MOW IRT statement that such individuals are comfortable recommending their field to their children as a career. Overall, as "duty-oriented social contributors," MIRI-U librarians fit the MOW pattern of exchanging skill, knowledge, and responsibility for socially generated satisfaction and average income. England and Whitely (1990, 101) summarize the category by making these observations about relationships between such individuals and their workplaces:

> The duty-oriented social contribution workers are rather highly committed to work and report high quality [in their] present work situations, average income, and high occupational satisfaction. They see their work as making a contribution to society and this seems to be an important value for them. The organization design issue posed by this group concerns how to best maintain the potential for social contribution through job assignments and work unit assignments which incorporate this [contribution] value. Real involvement and participation in important work issues and organizational support to keep them . . . seem to [be] beneficial practices.

Indeed, various job satisfaction studies of librarians support these comments and the close fit between MIRI-U librarians and the duty-oriented social contribution model (e.g., D'Elia 1979; Lynch and Verdin 1983, 1987).

Looking only at U.S. participants in the full MOW IRT study of 15,000 participants, MIRI-U librarians would seem to cluster with those Americans who define working as contributing to society, with very little compulsion or unpleasantness connected to that activity. In exchange for their contributions, individuals gain positive personal effect and identity. Importantly, they reflect a sense of obligation to society rather than an entitlement from society. England and Whitely (1990, 95) note that "this concept of working includes several ideal elements of professionals." It clearly represents the ideals the librarians associate with academic librarianship in a research university, as well as with their own primary work. Through their strong parallels with the duty-oriented social contribution worker, their reflection of professional values, and their work preferences, MIRI-U librarians demonstrate that their work is central to their self-identities and to their lives. As the MOW IRT (1987, 80-81) researchers note, "[it] may be important to one individual primarily because of what is received from working; to another, primarily because of what he or she invests in the process of working, or because of some combination of these rationales." There is no single a priori reason for this work centrality; rather, as has been seen throughout this book, it is the cluster of tasks, activities, values, and meanings that the librarians associate with their work that has made it central to their lives.

Change

In discussing the dynamics of change, Qvale (1988) notes that work content, context, and perhaps even the meaning people attach to work seem to be changing. He also observes that "basic values may be satisfied through several different work arrangements" (220). We have seen that work (especially primary work) occupies a place of major importance in MIRI-U librarians' lives and that the meanings and values they associate with academic librarianship in a research university environment yield for them rich, complex, and satisfying work lives. Because the meanings given to work are those that come from a shared social construction of work among the librarians, we can expect that as a community they will continue to rely on one another for various kinds of meaning and value setting. And from their absorption of electronic technology into work activities, we can be fairly confident of their continued ability to meet challenges that may alter their work, work arrangements, and work lives.

Can we generalize from MIRI-U librarians to those in other types and sizes of colleges and universities? We can in two senses. First, we have seen that many of the attributes MIRI-U librarians give to their work and lives at work are validated in studies of other librarians and of professionals in general, although particular personal achievements and struggles obviously belong to these librarians alone. Second, most of the challenges currently facing the MIRI-U library system are endemic throughout higher education. Critical issues that Arthur M. McAnally and Robert B. Downs first identified for research university libraries in 1973 are now shared with other types of academic libraries: general growth in enrollment, increased turnover in institutional presidencies, changes in learning approaches and research patterns, the continuing information explosion, hard financial times, new planning and budgeting processes, changing theories of management, and increasing control by governing boards. In 1989, directors from a range of academic libraries foresaw organizational challenges resulting from technological advances, especially a blurring of public and technical services lines, and shifts of roles among librarians, paraprofessionals, and clerical staff (De Klerk and Euster 1989). And the kinds of future-oriented challenges Virginia Tiefel (1995, 65) discussed are not confined to the research university alone:

• Libraries will no longer be the main information source for many [users].

• The library will be without walls and will have to respond to a wider and more diverse clientele.

• Libraries will become more access oriented, document delivery will become more important, and the size of libraries will become less important.

• Access to almost all information will be available at the user's workstation.

• Libraries will need flexibility, collaboration, diversity, and fluidity.

• These changes will encourage librarians to become more active participants in the scholarly/communication process.

• Librarians must focus on mission, not method, and become proactive. They must create a vision of the electronic library.

It is characteristic of people in organizations that they will always seek to reduce uncertainty, increase predictability and stability, and achieve orderliness (Salaman 1980). This is no less true in a time of change than it is in a time of stasis. Yet the ideal-type characteristics that Hage and Powers (1992) postulated for postindustrial roles are already part of the work identity of MIRI-U librarians. They, and other kinds of librarians, will inhabit a future where work is cognitive, complex, fluid, evolutionary

and uncertain, interconnected, and increasingly intangible in its knowledge and service nature (Hallett 1987, Howard 1995c). Following Abbott's
(1988) line of argument, the librarians still will be vulnerable to any fundamental changes in the objective character of librarianship, of academic
librarianship, and of their primary work. To continue involvement in this
future work world, librarians will have to maintain productive old skills
while developing new ones. They will have to continue adapting and using shared meanings and values to provide a sense of direction and conti-
nuity.

The MIRI-U librarians may represent many librarians who feel that
they are experiencing a transition—or perhaps a series of transitions. Budget
difficulties, staff decreases and role alterations, technological pressures,
and continuous change—all contribute to a sense of climbing a very steep
hill. Some of the librarians clearly coupled the term *transition* with that of
change. Now, however, an increasing number believe they have somehow
found their way "over the hump." Chris represents them:

> I think everything seems to be getting harder. There seems to
> be more and more to do all the time. I think it's a certain
> kind of level of exhaustion that sets in. . . . [Yet] I'm excited
> about the transitions that we're going through and the
> changes. So, personally, I feel like I'm there and maybe a
> little ahead. At least I'm thinking about it.

> Interviewer: Sixty percent through? 70 percent through?

> Chris: Sixty-five to 70 percent, yeah. More than fifty per-
> cent, definitely. . . . I think I've been able to step back and
> look at what's not going right and acknowledge that some-
> thing has to change. . . . I just have too many questions about
> things, I guess. It's hard to explain, but I think that's why I'm
> over the hump.

The fact that Chris has and continues to ask questions is encouraging, for as Hales (1980, 178) noted, "No knowledge is properly known
until its practical connections are known." This study of what it is like to
be an academic librarian in a research university in the mid-1990s indi-

cates that MIRI-U librarians (and perhaps the rest of us) have led, and will continue to lead, rich, complex, and uncertain, yet satisfying, work lives. We will continue to seek balance between the known and the unknown, the prevailing and the newly emerging work activities and perspectives. We will continue to meet and take on, as Ranganathan (1970, 180) said, "the problems of the future—including the immediate future which will begin on the next day."

Note
1. Apathetic Workers, Alienated Workers, Economic Workers, High Rights and Duties Economic Workers, Techno-Bureaucratic Workers, Duty-Oriented Social Contribution Workers, Work-Centered Expressive Workers, and Work-Centered and Balanced Workers.

Appendix

For the convenience of readers interested in background on the twenty-nine MIRI-U librarians interviewed for this study, this appendix begins with their 1994 profiles and then goes on to profile academic librarians in general. It concludes with a description of how I conducted the study that is the basis of this book.

MIRI-U Participants

The twenty-nine librarians comprise 36 percent of all MIRI-U librarians in positions below those considered administrative on the library's organizational chart. They come from reference, catalog, and collection units, as well as from various subject libraries such as archives and departmental libraries. They represent 33 percent of the MIRI-U librarians doing primarily collection work, 40 percent of those engaged in catalog work, and 36 percent of those in reference work. Women make up 72 percent of the participants (versus their 69 percent representation in the MIRI-U librarian population).

In addition to being interviewed and observed, the librarians responded to nine questions regarding their backgrounds that replicated Perry Morrison's (1969) study of the social origins, educational attainments, vocational experience, and personality characteristics of a group of American academic librarians. Their responses yielded the following:

1. The librarians have spent from three to twenty-nine years in their current positions at MIRI-U. The mean is nine and one half years; the mode is seven years.

2. Seventy-four percent spent a year or less between thinking about becoming a librarian and deciding to do so; the remaining 26 percent spent between three and ten years, during which time they held jobs that were usually related to work they now do as librarians. Fifty-two percent held other occupations before becoming librarians. These earlier jobs ranged from U.S. postal service employee to high school or college teacher to corporate scientist.

3. The MIRI-U librarians gave the following reasons for choosing librarianship. Several had more than one reason:
• liked previous experiences with libraries (39%);
• library work related to other interests (30%);
• wanted a career (22%);
• other jobs did not work out (17%);
• fellowships available (9%).

4. The librarians were between 21 and 40 years old when they received their master's in library science. The majority were in their twenties, with 29 being the average age. Current ages range from 29 to 63, with the mean being just under 50 years.

5. Fifty-seven percent hold advanced degrees. Including those actively pursuing a doctorate, eight have second master's degrees (biology, business, English, classics, history, liberal studies), and five have Ph.D.s (library and information science, American studies, history, and biology). As undergraduates, they earned degrees in these fields (first field only):

Humanities (13)	Social Sci. (5)	Natural/Physical Sciences (5)
English	Psychology	Biology
German	Geography	Zoology
History	International	
Music	Relations	

6. They responded as follows when asked what *two* statements express the main purposes of an undergraduate education (N=46; displayed in descending order of total participant response; %):

48   Develop one's critical faculties and appreciation of ideas
17   Develop one's knowledge of, and interest in, community and world problems
13   Provide vocational or pre-professional training; develop skills and techniques directly applicable to one's career
11   Develop special competence in a particular academic discipline
4   Help develop one's moral capacities, ethical standards and values
4   Other: Develop a broad background knowledge of one's own and other cultures; have fun
2   Develop one's ability to get along with different kinds of people.
--   Prepare for a happy marriage and family life

7. Most are involved in one or more professional associations, which form five clusters. In addition to general membership, several participants are actively involved in committees, councils, etc.:

Association	Membership (%)	Active (%)
ALA	61	50
ACRL	22	60
Special Libraries Association	30	14
State library association	39	100
Specialization-related association	57	54

8. Their parents completed a range of educational levels. The majority had attended college (N=23):

Level Attained	Mother (%)	Father (%)
1–8 grades	9	22
High school diploma	35	26
Some college	30 ⎫	17 ⎫
Bachelor's degree	9 ⎬ =56%	13 ⎬ = 51%
Master's degree	17 ⎭	4 ⎪
Doctorate	–	17 ⎭

9. When the librarians were high school juniors, their parents engaged in the following work. (I have broadened some participants' descriptive wording, for example combining school principal and college

professor under Educators.) Participants talked about twenty-three mothers and twenty-two fathers (N = 45):

Homemakers (8)	Physicians (2)
Office workers (7)	Service workers (2)
Farmers (5)	Social service workers (2)
Educators (4)	Other: Deceased (1)
Manufacturing workers (4)	In navy (1)
Salesmen (4)	On welfare (1)
Owner of business (3)	Unemployed (1)

Academic Librarians: 1969–1991

Several studies have sought to define the characteristics of librarians from a range of academic institutions (Morrison 1969; Schiller 1969; Massman 1972; Hitchingham 1986; Moran 1989; Cravey 1991). Their findings, plus review of ARL organization charts (1973, 1986, 1991), suggest a profile of the academic librarian and his or her work setting. Comparison of MIRI-U participants with the following broad summary of those 1969–1991 findings demonstrates that the MIRI-U librarians fit (and continue) this generalized portrait.

The typical academic librarian is a white, Protestant, married woman in her forties. Her parents are middle-class, white-collar workers or professionals of no particular wealth. Before becoming a librarian, she favored a humanities undergraduate major and believes the main purpose of a college education is to develop critical faculties and an appreciation for ideas. She chose librarianship as a career after graduating from college and received her master's degree in librarianship in her mid-twenties to early thirties. There is a one-in-three probability that she has, or is working on, a second graduate degree. The librarian believes in continuing education and belongs to at least one professional library association. She is above average in intelligence and on norm-referenced instruments scores average in terms of ability to supervise, take initiative, and demonstrate self-assurance.

This librarian probably has had some nonlibrary job experience at the professional, technical, or administrative level in an educational setting. She chose librarianship for a number of reasons: as an alternative to a previous occupation; in order to use previous training or experience; or because she was attracted to the atmosphere of libraries and the opportunity for service that librarianship offered. The librarian probably has worked in more than one academic library and has been in her current library for six to seven years.

She is highly satisfied with her choice of academic librarianship as a career, and is particularly pleased to provide service to inquirers, to build collections, and to work in what she defines as a stimulating environment with interesting colleagues. She likes problem-solving and specialized bibliographic work. The intellectual, technical, and precise nature of her work and the opportunity to learn and do research are also admired factors. Generally, she is accustomed to working with computers, but wants them to be even more user-friendly. She is likelier to work in a public area such as reference than in cataloging. She prefers that library support staff handle routine activities. Depending upon the employment requirements of her library and institution, she may spend increasing amounts of time pursuing some level of research leading to an occasional journal article or to publications within the library. The library and institutional committees on which she serves also have increased in number over the past few years. As an academic librarian, she sees herself as busy, professional, helpful, cooperative, competent, and knowledgeable.

Most frustrating to this librarian is having to do what she perceives as nonlibrarian, routine activities, especially as she believes that many tasks librarians used to handle can now be turned over to trained support staff. She also is not enamored of administrative detail and red tape, preferring flexible library work policies and opportunities for shared decision-making.

The library she works in is generally hierarchical in structure and arranged by library function. The 1950s organizational model, with work units grouped into technical services and public services, still prevails. Her library has separate reporting lines to the director for units such as collection development, preservation, automation, and personnel. She finds that a Friends of the Library group exists for raising money and hears talk of hiring a development officer to help with those efforts. There is also discussion of flattening out the pyramid by eliminating some assistant university librarian managerial positions. Her involvement in a librarians council or a staff advisory committee means that she interacts regularly with the director and several managerial librarians and that she is involved with some librarywide issues. Still, her own work area and set of responsibilities are where she enjoys spending most of her time and effort.

The Study

Researching academic librarians in the early 1990s, I found significant literature on academic *libraries* but a dearth of literature on academic *librarians*. There was a twofold result of this discovery. I conducted this study of a particular group of librarians and founded the nonprofit Center for the Study of Information Professionals, Inc., to carry out long-term, extensive research on all kinds of information professionals; royalties from this book will go to the center.

The question underlying the study was: What content and context do librarians in a public Research-I university ascribe to their work and work lives? Using distinctions made in *Policies for Life at Work* (OECD 1977), I divided "work" into job content and job context. "Job content" refers to tasks that collectively form a particular type of work. It encompasses the mental and physical demands of tasks, plus those resources necessary for the conduct of specific work. *Job context* refers to working conditions and workplace environment. *Work life* consists of work content and context in combination with each librarian's sense of where and when work is carried out.

Following Hall's dictum (1986, 13) that work is "a socially constructed phenomenon as well as an objective reality," I assumed librarians create an understanding of work and work life by vesting such phenomena with meaning. As an individual, each librarian assigns some sort of psychological symbol or mental construct to each happening she or he experiences. These symbols become recognized, expressed, and understood by the individual and thereby constitute "meaning." As members of a particular university, library system, and profession, the MIRI-U librarians reinforce meaningful actions and responses among themselves. The result is shared meaning.

In order to identify work- and work life-related meanings of participating librarians, I focused on values and preferences they give to work and work life concepts. Value and preference are bearers of meaning (after Hill 1971), with the former associated with establishing the worth of a thing and the latter indicating degrees of desirability regarding it. Taken together, meanings, values, and preferences give substance to librarians' work and work life constructs. Finally, because the participants were all academic librarians, I assumed that their constructs included assumptions and principles reflecting meanings, values, and preferences shared by members of that particular professional community.

Method

In order to ascertain personal and shared constructs, I needed to derive from the librarians themselves how they envision their work and work lives. This called for selecting a qualitative research method. Bogdan and Biklen (1992) note that qualitative methods use the natural setting as the direct source of data and the researcher as the key instrument for gathering them. They find that qualitative research is primarily descriptive with major attention given to meanings, values, and preferences, and that qualitative researchers are concerned with process rather than simply outcomes or products. Such researchers also tend to analyze their data inductively, and meaning is of essential concern (31–33).

From among the various qualitative methods available, I chose to use the constant comparative approach of grounded theory because it supported the study's design requirements. First, the most intimate expression of meaning, values, and preferences comes in the words librarians use when discussing work and work life. Deriving concepts from words indicated the value of open-ended questions and face-to-face interactions. Second, the study required identifying similarities, differences, and degrees of consistency of meaning. This indicated a need for flexibility in data collection, coding, and analysis. Third, the method had to support experiential data because it would be impossible to set aside completely my own previous experiences as an academic librarian in Research-I university settings.

As first presented by Barney G. Glaser and Anselm L. Strauss (1967) and later explicated by Anselm Strauss and Juliet Corbin (1990), this method uses a variety of qualitative data collection techniques and exhibits four overlapping stages that move from focusing on data incidents and emergence of categories to refinement of categories and articulation of theory. In the first stage, stated research questions guide data collection. For example, I asked each librarian to "tell me what you do." This very open-ended question elicited personal representations or depictions of what they chose to see as their work, rather than my assumptions about what their work included and entailed. Analysis of data collected through techniques such as open-ended interviews, documents, and field observation identifies specific data incidents. The researcher codes like incidents as similar and associates them with each other through formulating and refining categories. Thus, references to being able to select what tasks to do, and when, might be coded as "choosing." Constant comparison of each successive datum with previous data builds categories not constrained to a preset number, but reflecting, instead, the diversity of the data and data collection techniques. The coding process is central to analysis as it identifies underlying patterns in data. As a category takes on substance (i.e., emerges from data), the researcher becomes aware of its theoretical properties: dimensions, relationship to other categories, and conditions that add to or subtract from it.

The second stage of the constant comparative method focuses on comparing data incidents with properties of emergent categories. In this stage, the researcher minimizes differences between sources of data incidents, thereby producing maximum similarity in data. For instance, a number of librarians mention having autonomy. This seems to be similar to the choosing code word. Both seem to refer to the ability to make independent decisions about work: when, where, how, why. This maximizing approach to coding results in integration of categories and their properties, and thus analysis moves from empirical toward conceptual and theoretical levels. In our example, autonomy seems a broader concept than does choosing, so the latter is incorporated as part of an enlarged notion of the former. As an emerging concept, autonomy pulls together notions of personal choice within one's own set of activities, the idea of structuring one's own day, and the expression of "feeling free."

Continuing analysis and further refinement of concepts and their relationships gradually lead to development of a tentative theory, which is delimited in the third stage of the method. For instance, what is the relationship between the emerging concept of autonomy and that of another concept I have labeled "deliberate actions"? Are the two the same, or overlapping, or distinctly different? At this point, the researcher initiates theoretical sampling: Decisions about what additional data to collect rest on the potential theoretical relevance of data for further development of emerging categories. As tentative theory guides the choice of data sources, the researcher maximizes differences among those sources. This, in turn, leads to dense development of category properties and delimitation of the theory's scope. I find that autonomy and deliberate actions are distinct, with both being part of a larger, more theoretical concept I label "exercising choice."

The process of data collection and analysis ends when all major concepts and their interrelationships are theoretically saturated, that is, when the researcher finds that additional data do not further develop existing categories or embellish theory. Presentation of theory in discussion format or as a set of propositions constitutes the final stage of the constant comparative method.

This research approach does not use a predetermined design for data collection and analysis. Instead, the researcher continually redesigns the investigation as concepts, their properties and interrelationships gradually emerge, develop, and are refined. As data collection, coding, and analysis progress, the researcher is able to refute certain concepts, eliminate those with insufficient support, and modify some and validate others. Through use of theoretical sampling, the focus shifts from stressing similarities to stressing differences between data sources until resulting concepts exhibit theoretical saturation. The result is a grounded theory based on, and validated by, empirical evidence.

The Site

To protect the confidentiality of participants, I named the site Midwest Public Research-I University (MIRI-U). A multicampus institution founded in the mid-1800s, it enrolls more than 30,000 undergraduates and graduates. In addition to the university, names of the library facilities, units, and participants are pseudonymous.

Three library facilities warrant names. I refer to the one housing a number of centralized departments, library administrative offices, and a significant amount of the overall collection as the Humanities and Social Sciences Library (HSS). A counterpart science library with its own departments, offices, and collection is called science library. The medical library, although a part of the medical college, has formal association with the library system. A number of departmental libraries also exist. Within the major library buildings are numerous topical collections. Each has a unit head and staff; each is semiautonomous, conducting its own collection building and user services activities. These are referred to as subject libraries to distinguish them from the general units and services of the library building in which they are located.

Participating Librarians

I reduced to approximately ninety the individuals MIRI-U considers "librarians" by omitting those defined as administrative on the library's organizational chart. Following Schiller (1969) and other researchers, I assumed that at MIRI-U these librarians would engage primarily in organizational activities related to budgeting, evaluation, and strategic planning. Their elimination does not mean that the remaining librarians do no managing or administering, but this responsibility is not as likely to dominate their work.

To obtain a wide range and richness of data incidents reflecting meanings, values, and preferences about work and work life, I sought a diverse set of participants. Seeking diversity in gender, ethnicity, age, and years of experience in the MIRI-U library makes theoretical sense but is secondary to the diversity of work being sought. Although the constant comparative method does not require preset numbers or random selection of participants, inclusion of individuals from areas that potentially are theoretically relevant to the research question is necessary. Using various approaches, I contacted librarians from all units and across the major library buildings. Inititally, twenty librarians responded through written and e-mail correspondence; nine others became participants through on-site recommendations and interactions. During data collection, I determined that these volunteers actually were a representative sample of the work variety found in MIRI-U's library system, as well as of participant age, years of library experience, and gender. After on-site observation and review of staff lists, I chose not to seek ethnic or racial diversity; librarians at MIRI-U are overwhelmingly caucasian. The next largest ethnic groups are Arab and Asian, who together comprise less than five percent of all librarians and work in fewer than five specific locations.

Data Collection, Coding, and Analysis

I collected data through interviews, observation, and journal-keeping. This triangulation of sources resulted in a deeper and clearer understanding of the perspectives of the librarians. I conducted four weeks of on-site interviews from March through May 1994; one week on-site was followed by two weeks off-site. Final analysis and initial written description of the findings took a year.

I conducted individual, face-to-face, open-ended, taped interviews with twenty-three participants: the original twenty volunteers and three of those who became participants during site visits. I took notes during conversations with five others. I count one more as participating, although I made notes only after our conversation. Because the objective was to identify work content and context as the *librarians* viewed them, interviews were loosely structured: I asked participants the same initial questions and used their comments to derive additional questions. Individualization of each interview enabled the librarians to add depth to their own particular work life characterizations. Use of consistent questions helped ensure some comparable data across sites and participants.

Observation was also used. An interview is its own event and, as such, does not rule out possible discrepancy between what someone says and actually does, or says in an interview setting and then remembers more completely in his or her actual work setting (Taylor and Bogdan 1984; Hammersley and Atkinson 1983). Observing participants in their work setting allows validation of assumptions and development of context within which to understand an individual's statement or perspective (Schatzman and Strauss 1973; Marshall and Rossman 1989). Such engagement encourages a conversational situation that treats topics as they develop. Finally, observation provides a real-time medium in which to pursue leads from interviews, explore participants' interests, and gain a more complete sense of tasks, work systems, and working conditions. So, when I did not understand their perspective on certain tasks, I asked participants to "walk me through" their work. I observed various work activities of six librarians and spent time as a "complete observer" (Hammersley and Atkinson 1983) in five public and one staff-only areas, having had no contact with participants prior to interviewing them.

On seven randomly chosen days, four participants kept journals in which they commented in whatever way they wished on the day just concluded. The journals provide enriching information and assist in confirming or disconfirming activities, meanings, and preferences previously espoused by librarians or construed as such by me (Hammersley and

Atkinson 1983). Journal-keeping also offered participants opportunities for reflection. Journal keepers were selected serendipitously as I came across individuals who I believed might provide additional depth of thought through a journal.

Initial interview questions were developed by drawing from Friedmann and Havighurst (1954), Dan C. Lortie (1975), James P. Spradley (1979), Pamela J. Cravey (1991), the MOW International Research Team (1987), and Corrine Glesne and Alan Peshkin (1992), framing them within the question types of Michael Quinn Patton (1990) and Spradley (1979) and associating the result with meaning, values, and preferences definitions. The last step allowed me finally to select and pretest specific open-ended questions.

Coding and Analysis
In the constant comparative method, coding begins when data collection begins and analysis begins when association is made between two or more codes. Constantly comparing data incidents results in continuous interplay between data collection, coding, and analysis. Interviews were taped, while I actively listened—encouraging conversation, following up on comments, adding questions beyond the interview schedule, and trying to ensure that I understood what the participant was conveying. A profile sheet was subsequently developed for each individual, including personal appearance and characteristics, the interview setting, general impressions, and any detail that might help me remember this person. Disk transcriptions were made by a professional transcriber. Coding focused on identifying as many potentially relevant categories as possible. I worked with the transcripts to identify potential trends, possible themes, and new perspectives, and thus to shape additional questions for subsequent interviews. Initially, I did not keep a list of the code words, preferring to respond directly to each data incident as I found it in the transcribed text. As soon as coding suggested categories I could tentatively name, I began keeping a code list and introduced theoretical sampling into data collection by enlarging my interview questions to include those suggested by emerging categories. At that point, coding shifted so that it related more specifically to emerging categories and subcategories, and I sought evidence of variation and distinction among categories.

During this phase, discerning differences between librarians on the basis of work area or task was minimally important. The emphasis on similarity supported the generation of basic categories and their properties. However, as fewer and fewer new categories emerged, I used theoretical sampling to maximize differences between categories. Prior to the final on-site visit, I compared participants' basic demographic data against what I knew about all MIRI-U librarians and participant work areas against all MIRI-U library work areas to "stretch diversity of data as far as possible, just to make certain that saturation [was] based on the widest possible range of data" (Glaser and Strauss 1967, 61). Both theoretical sampling and saturation led me to conclude that I had empirically based category properties.

To support the process of developing, refuting, eliminating, and refining concepts, I used *The Ethnograph*, a set of interactive, menu-driven programs designed primarily for ethnographic and qualitative research. The software enables researchers to code, record, and sort textual data files into analytic categories (called data segments). Coding schemes can be revised and modified through additions and deletions of codes. Data segments are searchable by single or multiple code words. After transferring assigned codes into the online program, I reviewed text, marked code segments and displayed, sorted, and printed various segments, facilitating interpretation and comparison of segments with either each other or differently categorized segments. Being able, at any time, to revise codes allowed me to impose new and larger conceptual representations onto data as such arose. It was here, for instance, that I saw "choosing" become part of the larger concept of autonomy. *The Ethnograph* can produce both alphabetical and frequency lists reflecting all of the codes a researcher assigns throughout a file. After coding participant interviews and profile sheets, I merged alphabetical code lists to create a master list containing over two hundred code words representing subcategories and categories. Analyzing code segments resulted in various codes melding into emerging categories; others remained unique to specific participants.

In addition, I used parts of Strauss and Corbin's (1990) paradigm model to increase the density and precision of both concepts and tentative theory. The steps in this model expose relationships between subcategories and categories, and between categories. For a selected (sub)category, the model considers its causal conditions, properties, and dimensions, as well as intervening conditions that act upon it, strategies for meeting those conditions, and consequences related to such actions and strategies. Thus, I used the properties and dimensions steps to refine the autonomy and the deliberate actions categories. These steps served as the basis for standard qualitative analytic and theoretical memos, and diagrams reflecting concepts. The resulting larger concepts, such as that of exercising choice, represented how participating librarians envision their work and work lives. These final concepts are deeply developed, exhibit strong internal relationships, and are clear enough for subsequent qualitative or quantitative testing.

Assumptions and Limitations
Three assumptions underlie this study: (1) An individual's work life is a reality constructed by that individual through development and adoption of meanings, values, and preferences; (2) this reality is generally shared with others in the same work setting; (3) drawing together work content and context perceptions of MIRI-U participants enables a composite work life portrait of librarians at that university to be painted.

At the same time, the study has limitations: (1) This is a slice-of-time study, and the final portrait is not necessarily generalizable to either previous or future portrayals of a public Research-I academic librarian's work life; (2) the portrait is not necessarily generalizable beyond MIRI-U; (3) limiting eligibility to librarians below the level of administrators means the findings may not reflect the work or work lives of librarians at that level.

The data obtained depended on the willingness of participants to reflect upon their work—its content and context—and to decipher their work life for me. Ultimately, the study is also limited by the extent to which I failed to see through their eyes and walk in their shoes.

Bibliography

Abbott, Andrew. 1988. *The system of professions: An essay on the division of expert labor.* Chicago: Univ. of Chicago Pr.

Abell, Millicent D. 1979. The changing role of the academic librarian: drift and mastery. In *New horizons for academic libraries: Papers presented at the First National Conference of the Association of College and Research Libraries, Boston, Massachusetts, November 8–11, 1978,* ed. Robert D. Stueart and Richard D. Johnson, 66–78. New York: K. G. Saur.

Adamany, David W. 1985. Research libraries from a presidential perspective. In *Issues in academic librarianship: Views and case studies for the 1980s and 1990s,* ed. Peter Spyers-Duran and Thomas W. Mann Jr., 5–20. New York: Greenwood.

Adler, Paul. 1984. Tools for resistance: Workers can make automation their ally. *Dollars and Sense* 100 (Oct.): 7–8.

ALA yearbook: A review of library events 1977. Vol. 3. 1978. Chicago: ALA.

Alafiatayo, Benjamin O., Yau J. Yip, and John C. P. Blunden-Ellis. 1996. Reference transaction and the nature of the process for general reference assistance. *Library & Information Science Research* 18 (fall): 357–84.

Algera, Jen A. 1990. The job characteristics model of work motivation revisited. In *Work Motivation,* ed. Uwe Kleinbeck, Hans-Henning Quast, Henk Thierry, and Hartmut Hacker, 85–104. Hillsdale, N.J.: Lawrence Erlbaum Associates.

Allen, Gillian. 1993. An application of the act frequency approach in the study of person-job fit. *Library & Information Science Research* 15 (summer): 249–55.

Alsalam, Nabeel, and Gayle Thompson Rogers, eds. 1990. *The condition of education, 1990. Volume 2: Postsecondary education.* Washington, D.C.: National Center for Education Statistics.

American Library Association. 1970. *Library education and manpower: A statement of policy adopted by the Council of the American Library Association, June 30, 1970.* Chicago: ALA.

American library directory, 1980: 33rd edition. New York: R.R. Bowker.

American library directory, 1991–92: 43rd edition. New York: R.R. Bowker.

American library directory, 1993–94: 46th edition. New Providence, N.J.: R.R. Bowker.

Applebaum, Herbert. 1992. *The concept of work: Ancient, medieval, and modern.* SUNY series in the anthropology of work. Albany, N.Y.: State Univ. of New York Pr..

Argyle, Michael. 1972. *The social psychology of work.* New York: Taplinger.

ARL Statistics, 1981–82. Washington, D.C.: ARL.

ARL Statistics, 1990–91. Washington, D.C.: ARL.

ARL Statistics, 1991–92. Washington, D.C.: ARL.

Asher, Robert. 1995. Work skill in historical perspective. In *The new modern times: Factors reshaping the world of work,* ed. David B. Bills 51–79. SUNY series in the sociology of work. Albany, N.Y.: State Univ. of New York Pr.

Association of Research Libraries, Office of Management Services, Systems and Procedures Exchange Center. 1973. *Organization charts.* SPEC Kit 1. Washington, D.C.: ARL.

Association of Research Libraries, Office of Management Services, Systems and Procedures Exchange Center. 1985. *Automation and reorganization of technical and public services.* SPEC Kit 112. Washington, D.C.: ARL.

Association of Research Libraries, Office of Management Services, Systems and Procedures Exchange Center. 1986. *Organization charts.* SPEC Kit 129. Washington, D.C.: ARL.

Association of Research Libraries, Office of Management Services, Systems and Procedures Exchange Center. 1991. *Organization charts in ARL libraries.* SPEC Kit 170. Washington, D.C.: ARL.

Baldridge, J. Victor, David V. Curtis, George P. Ecker, and Gary L. Riley. 1977. Alternative models of governance in higher education. In *ASHE reader on organization and governance in higher education,* ed. Marvin

W. Peterson, 11–27. Needham Heights, Mass.: Ginn Pr.. Reprint from Baldridge, Victor J., and Gary L. Riley, eds. *Governing American organizations: New problems, new perspectives.* (year?). Berkeley, Calif.: McCutchan.

Baumeister, Roy F. 1991. *Meanings of life.* New York: Guilford.

Becker, Howard S., and Blanche Geer. 1958. Participant-observation and interviewing: A comparison. *Human Organization* 16 (3): 28–32.

Bell, Daniel. 1973. *The coming of post-industrial society.* New York: Basic Bks.

Bem, Daryl J. 1970. *Beliefs, attitudes, and human affairs.* Belmont, Calif.: Brooks/Cole.

Bensimon, Estela M., Anna Neumann, and Robert Birnbaum. 1989. *Making sense of administrative leadership: The 'L' word in higher education.* ASHE-ERIC higher education report 1. Washington, D.C.: School of Education and Human Development, George Washington Univ.

Berger, Peter L., and Thomas Luckmann. 1966. *The social construction of reality: A treatise in the sociology of knowledge.* New York: Doubleday.

Bergquist, William H. 1992. *The four cultures of the academy: Insights and strategies for improving leadership in collegiate organizations.* San Francisco: Jossey-Bass.

Bills, David B., ed. 1995. *The new modern times: Factors reshaping the world of work.* SUNY series in the sociology of work. Albany, N.Y.: State Univ. of New York Pr..

Birnbaum, Robert. 1988. *How colleges work: The cybernetics of academic organization and leadership.* San Francisco: Jossey-Bass.

Blackburn, Robert T. and Janet H. Lawrence. 1995. *Faculty at work: Motivation, expectation, satisfaction.* Baltimore: The Johns Hopkins Univ. Pr.

Blankenship, Ralph L., ed. 1977. *Colleagues in organization: The social construction of professional work.* New York: Wiley.

Blauner, Robert. 1964. *Alienation and freedom.* Chicago: Univ. of Chicago Pr..

Bledstein, Burton J. 1976. *The culture of professionalism: The middle class and the development of higher education in America.* New York: W. W. Norton.

Bogdan, Robert C., and Sari Knopp Biklen. 1992. *Qualitative research for education: An introduction to theory and methods.* 2nd ed. Boston: Allyn and Bacon.

Bolman, Lee G., and Terrence E. Deal. 1997. *Reframing organizations: Artistry, choice, and leadership.* 2nd ed. San Francisco: Jossey-Bass.

Branin, Joseph J. 1991. Cooperative collection development. In *Collection management: A new treatise,* ed. Charles Osburn and Ross Atkinson, 81–110. Greenwich, Conn.: JAI.

Braude, Lee. 1983. *Work and workers: A sociological analysis.* Malabar, Fla.: Robert E. Krieger.

Braverman, Harry. 1974. *Labor and monopoly capital.* New York: Monthly Review Pr..

Brenner, Patricia E. 1984. *Stress and satisfaction on the job: Work meanings and coping of mid-career men.* New York: Praeger Special Studies.

Brief, Arthur P., and Walter R. Nord, eds. 1990. *Meanings of occupational work: A collection of essays.* Lexington, Mass.: Lexington Bks.

Brough, Kenneth J. 1953. *Scholar's workshop: Evolving conceptions of library service.* Illinois contributions to librarianship, no. 5. Urbana, Ill.: Univ. of Illinois Pr..

Brubacher, John S., and Willis Rudy. 1976. *Higher education in transition: A history of American colleges and universities, 1636–1976.* 3rd ed. New York: Harper & Row.

Buckland, Michael K. 1989. Foundations of academic librarianship. *College & University Libraries* 50 (July): 389–96.

Bunge, Charles A. 1984. Interpersonal dimensions of the reference interview: A historical review of the literature." *Drexel Library Quarterly* 20 (2): 4–23.

———. 1980. Reference services. In *ALA world encyclopedia of library and information services.* 1st ed., 468–74. Chicago: ALA.

Burawoy, Michael. 1979. *Manufacturing consent.* Chicago: Univ. of Chicago Pr..

Butler, Pierce. 1951. Librarianship as a profession. *Library Quarterly* 21 (Oct.): 235–47.

Canelas, Dale Brunelle. 1971. *Task analysis of library jobs in the state of Illinois: A working paper on the relevance of the study to academic libraries.* ERIC ED 067 113. Washington, D.C.: U.S. Dept. of Health, Education and Welfare.

Caplow, Theodore. 1954. *The sociology of work.* Minneapolis: Univ. of

Minnesota Pr..

Chan, Lois Mai. 1994. *Cataloging and classification.* 2nd ed. New York: McGraw Hill.

Cherrington, David J. 1980. *The work ethic: Working values and values that work.* New York: AMACOM.

Chiang, Win-Shin S., and Nancy E. Elkington, eds. *Electronic access to information: A new service paradigm.* Mountain View, Calif.: Research Libraries Group.

Childers, Thomas, Cynthia Lopata, and Brian Stafford. 1991. Measuring the difficulty of reference questions. *RQ* 31 (winter): 237–43.

Clark, Burton R. 1987. *The academic life: Small worlds, different worlds.* Princeton, N.J.: Carnegie Foundation for the Advancement of Teaching.

Classification of institutions of higher education. 1973. Berkeley, Calif.: Carnegie Commission on Higher Education.

Classification of institutions of higher education. 1987. A Carnegie Foundation technical report. 3rd ed. Princeton, N.J.: Princeton Univ. Pr..

Cohen, Michael D., and James G. March. 1986. *Leadership and ambiguity: The American college president.* 2nd ed. Boston: Harvard Business School Pr.

Connaway, Lynn Silipigni. 1992. The levels of decisions and involvement in decision-making: Effectiveness and job satisfaction in academic library technical services. (Ph.D. diss., Univ. of Wisconsin-Madison).

Conrad, Clifton F. 1978. A grounded theory of academic change." *Sociology of Education* 51: 101–12.

Cravey, Pamela J. 1991. Occupational role identity of women academic librarians. *College & Research Libraries* 52 (Mar.): 150–64.

Creelman, Marjorie B. 1966. *The experimental investigation of meaning: A review of the literature.* New York: Springer.

Creth, Sheila D. 1989. Personnel issues for academic librarians: A review and perspectives for the future. *College & Research Libraries* 50 (Mar.): 144–52.

Cummings, Anthony M., Marcia L. Witte, William G. Bowen, Laura O. Lazarus, and Richard H. Ekman. 1992. *University libraries and scholarly communication: A study prepared for the Andrew W. Mellon Foundation.* Washington, D.C.: ARL.

Czander, William M. 1993. *The psychodynamics of work and organiza-*

tions: Theory and application. New York: Guilford Pr..

Darrah, Charles N. 1996. *Learning and work: An exploration in industrial ethnography.* New York: Garland.

De Cock, Gaston. 1986. What organizational psychologists say they do and what they really do. In *The psychology of work and organization,* eds. G. Debus and H.-W. Schroiff, 367–78. Amsterdam: Elsevier Science.

de Gennaro, Richard. 1975. Austerity, technology and resource sharing. *Library Journal* 100 (May): 917–23.

de Keyser, Veronique, Thoralf Qvale, Bernhard Wilpert, and S. Antonio Ruiz Quintanilla, eds. 1988. *The meaning of work and technological options.* New technologies and work series. Chichester, Eng.: Wiley.

de Klerk, Ann, and Joanne R. Euster. 1989. Technology and organizational metamorphoses. *Library Trends* 37 (spring): 457–68.

D'Elia, George P. 1979. The determinants of job satisfaction among beginning librarians." *Library Quarterly* 49 (July): 283–302.

Des Chene, Dorice. 1985. Online searching by end users." *RQ* 25 (1): 89–95.

Dewey, Melvil. 1976. The profession. In *Landmarks of library literature, 1876–1976,* ed. Dianne J. Ellsworth and Norman D. Stephens, 21–23. Metuchen, N.J.: Scarecrow. Reprinted from *Library Journal,* 1 (1) (Sept. 30, 1876).

Digest of Educational Statistics, 1973. Washington, D.C.: Department of Health, Education, and Welfare.

Digest of Education Statistics, 1982. Washington, D.C.: National Center for Education Statistics.

Digest of Education Statistics, 1991. Washington, D.C.: National Center for Education Statistics.

Digest of Education Statistics, 1993. Washington, D.C.: National Center for Education Statistics.

Douglass, Robert Raymond. 1957. The personality of the librarian. (Ph.D. diss., University of Chicago). Referenced in Pauline Wilson, *Stereotype and status: Librarians in the United States* (Westport, Conn.: Greenwood), 9.

Downs, Robert B. 1976. The role of the academic librarian, 1876–1976. In *Libraries for teaching, libraries for research: Essays for a century,* ed. Richard D. Johnson. ACRL publications in librarianship, no. 39: 115–

26. Chicago: ALA.

Du Gay, Paul. 1996. *Consumption and identity at work.* London: Sage.

Dubeck, Paula J. and Kathryn Borman, eds. 1996. *Women and work: A handbook.* New York: Garland.

Dubin, Robert. 1956. Industrial workers' worlds: A study of the "central life interests" of industrial workers." *Social Problems* 3 (Jan.): 131–42.

Edelman, Hendrik, and G. Marvin Tatum Jr. 1976. The development of collections in American university libraries. In *Libraries for teaching, libraries for research: Essays for a century,* ed. Richard D. Johnson. ACRL publications in librarianship, no. 39: 34–57. Chicago: ALA. Reprinted from *College & Research Libraries* 37 (May 1976): 222–45.

Edwards, Ralph M. 1975. *The role of the beginning librarian in university libraries.* ACRL publications in librarianship, no. 37. Chicago: ALA.

Encyclopaedia Britannica, 15th ed., s.v. "history of the organization of work."

England, George W. 1988. The variety of work meanings—USA, Germany and Japan. In *The meaning of work and technological options,* ed. Veronique De Keyser, Thoralf Qvale, Bernhard Wilpert, and S. Antonio Ruiz Quintanilla, 37–44. Chichester, Eng.: Wiley.

England, George W. and William T. Whitely. 1990. *Post-industrial lives: Roles and relationships in the 21st century.* Newbury Park, Calif.: Sage.

Epstein, Seymour. 1989. Values from the perspective of cognitive-experiential self-theory. In *Social and moral values: Individual and societal perspectives,* ed. Nancy Eisenberg, Janusz Reykowski, and Ervin Staub, 3–22. Hillsdale, N.J.: Lawrence Erlbaum.

Erikson, Kai. 1990. Introduction. In *The nature of work: Sociological perspectives,* ed. Kai Erikson and Steven Peter Vallas, 1–15. New Haven, Conn.: Yale Univ. Pr..

Estabrook, Leigh. 1989. The growth of the profession. *College & Research Libraries* 50 (May): 287–96.

Evans, G. Edward. 1983. *Management techniques for librarians.* 2nd ed. Orlando, Fla.: Academic Pr.

Farber, Evan Ira. 1995. Bibliographic instruction, briefly. In *Information for a new age: Redefining the librarian,* comp. by the Fifteenth Anniversary Task Force, Library Instruction Round Table, ALA, 23–34. Englewood, Colo.: Libraries Unlimited.

Finkelstein, Martin J. 1984. *The American academic profession: A synthesis of social scientific inquiry since World War II.* Columbus, Ohio: Ohio State Univ. Pr..

Fisher, Kimball. 1994. Diagnostic issues for work teams. In *Diagnosis for Organizational Change: Methods and Models,* ed. Howard, Ann and Associates, 239–64. New York: Guilford Pr..

Ford, Julienne. 1975. *Paradigms and fairy tales: An introduction to the science of meanings.* 2 vol. London: Routledge & Kegan Paul.

Frankie, Suzanne O. 1980. The behavioral styles, work preferences and values of an occupational group: A study of university catalog and reference librarians." (D.P.A. diss., George Washington Univ.).

———. 1982. Occupational characteristics of university librarianship: A study of university catalog and reference librarians. In *Options for the 80s: Proceedings of the Second National Conference of the Association of College and Research Libraries,* ed. Michael D. Kathman and Virgil F. Massman, 405–11. Greenwich, Conn.: JAI.

Freidson, Eliot, ed. 1973. *The professions and their prospects.* Beverly Hills, Calif.: Sage.

Freidson, Eliot. 1986. *Professional powers: A study of the institutionalization of formal knowledge.* Chicago: Univ. of Chicago Pr..

Freidson, Eliot. 1994. *Professionalism reborn: Theory, prophecy, and policy.* Chicago: Univ. of Chicago Pr.

Friedmann, Eugene A., and Robert J. Havighurst. 1954. *The meaning of work and retirement.* Chicago: Univ. of Chicago Pr..

Gamst, Frederick C. 1995. *Meanings of work: Considerations for the twenty-first century.* SUNY series in the anthropology of work. Albany, N.Y.: State Univ. of New York Pr..

Garrison, Dee. 1979. *Apostles of culture: The public librarian and American society, 1876–1920.* New York: Free Pr..

Geer, Blanche. 1970. Studying a college. In *Pathways to data: Field methods for studying ongoing social organizations,* ed. Robert W. Habenstein. Chicago: Aldine.

Geiger, Roger L. 1993. "Research universities in a new era: From the 1980s to the 1990s. In *Higher learning in America, 1980–2000,* ed. Arthur Levine, 67–85. Baltimore: John Hopkins Univ. Pr..

Gioia, Dennis A. 1986. Symbols, scripts, and sensemaking: Creating meaning in the organizational experience. In *The thinking organiza-*

tion, ed. Henry P. Sims Jr., Dennis A. Gioia, and Associates, 49–74. San Francisco: Jossey-Bass.

Gioia, Dennis A., and Poole, P. P. 1984. "Scripts in organizational behavior." *Academy of Management Review* 9 (3): 449–59.

Glaser, Barney G., and Anselm L. Strauss. 1967. *The discovery of grounded theory: Strategies for qualitative research*. Hawthorne, New York: Aldine de Gruyter.

Glesne, Corrine, and Alan Peshkin. 1992. *Becoming qualitative researchers: AniIntroduction*. White Plains, N.Y.: Longman.

Goetz, Judith Preissle, and Margaret Diane LeCompte. 1984. *Ethnography and qualitative design in educational research*. San Diego: Academic Pr..

Gross, Edward. 1958. *Work and society*. New York: Thomas Y. Crowell.

Guba, Egon G., and Yvonna S. Lincoln. 1981. *Effective evaluation: Improving the usefulness of evaluation results through responsive and naturalistic approaches*. San Francisco: Jossey-Bass.

Haber, Samuel. 1991. *The quest for authority and honor in the American professions, 1750–1900*. Chicago: Univ. of Chicago Pr..

Hackman, J. Richard. 1986. The psychology of self-management in organizations. In *Psychology and work: productivity, change, and employment*, ed. Robert Perloff and J. Richard Hackman, 85–136. Washington, D.C.: American Psychological Association.

Hackman, J. Richard, and Greg R. Oldham. 1980. *Work redesign*. Addison-Wesley's organization development series. Reading, Mass.: Addison-Wesley.

Hafter, Ruth. 1986. *Academic librarians and cataloging networks: Visibility, quality, control, and professional status*. Contributions in librarianship and information science, no. 57. New York: Greenwood.

Hage and Powers. 1992.

Hales, Mike. 1980. *Living thinkwork: Where do labour processes come from?* London: CSE Bks.

Hall, Richard H. 1986. *Dimensions of work*. Beverly Hills, Calif.: Sage.

Hallett, Jeffrey J. 1987. *Worklife visions: Redefining work for the information economy*. Alexandria, Va.: American Society for Personnel Administration.

Hamlin, Arthur T. 1981. *The university library in the United States: Its origins and development*. Philadelphia: Univ. of Pennsylvania Pr..

Hammersley, Martyn, and Paul Atkinson. 1983. *Ethnography: Principles in practice*. London: Routledge.

Harris, Michael H. 1986. State, class, and cultural reproduction: Toward a theory of library service in the United States. *Advances in Librarianship* 14: 211–52.

Harris, Roma M. 1992. *Librarianship: The erosion of a woman's profession*. Norwood, N.J.: Ablex.

The HEP 1992 Higher Education Directory. 1992. Washington, D.C.: Higher Education Publications.

Hearn, Stephen. 1994. Authority control. In *Guide to technical services resources*, ed. Peggy Johnson, 86–103. Chicago: ALA.

Hermans, Hubert J. M. 1990. Who shares whose values: Identity and motivation in organizations. In *Work motivation*, ed. Uwe Kleinbeck, Hans-Henning Quast, Henk Thierry, and Hartmut Hacker, 247–56. Hillsdale, N.J.: Lawrence Erlbaum.

Herzberg, Frederick, Bernard Mausner, and Barbara Bloch Snyderman. 1959. *The motivation to work*. 2nd ed. New York: Wiley.

Hewitt, Joe A., and John S. Shipman. 1987. Cooperative collection development among research libraries in the age of networking: Report of a survey of ARL libraries. *Advances in Library Automation and Networking* 1: 189–232.

Hill, Janet Swan. 1994. Descriptive cataloging. In *Guide to technical services resources*, ed. Peggy Johnson, 45–67. Chicago: ALA.

Hill, Thomas E. 1971. *The concept of meaning*. New York: Humanities Pr.

Hirschhorn, Larry. 1984. *Beyond mechanization*. Cambridge, Mass.: MIT Pr.

Hitchingham, Eileen E. 1986. Academic librarians' workload. In *Energies for transition: Proceedings of the Fourth National Conference of the Association of College and Research Libraries, Baltimore, Maryland, April 9–12, 1986*, ed. Danuta A. Nitecki, 133–38. Chicago: ALA.

Hodson, Randy. 1995. The worker as active subject: Enlivening the "new sociology of work." In *The new modern times: Factors reshaping the world of work*, ed. David B. Bills, 253–80. SUNY series in the sociology of work. Albany, N.Y.: State Univ. of New York Pr..

Holley, Edward G. 1976. Academic libraries in 1876. In *Libraries for teaching, libraries for research: Essays for a century*, ed. Richard D. Johnson. ACRL publications in librarianship no. 39, 1–33. Chicago: ALA.

Reprinted from *College & Research Libraries* 37 (Jan. 1976): 15–47.

Howard, Ann, ed. 1995a. *The changing nature of work*. San Francisco: Jossey-Bass.

———. 1995b. A framework for work change. In *The changing nature of work*, ed. Ann Howard, 1–44. San Francisco: Jossey-Bass.

———. 1995c. Rethinking the psychology of work. In *The changing nature of work*, ed. Ann Howard, 513–55. San Francisco: Jossey-Bass.

Hughes, Everett Cherrington. 1951. Work and Self. In *Social psychology at the crossroads*, ed. John H. Rohrer and Muzafer Sherif, 313–23. New York: Harper.

Hurowitz, Robert, and David R. McDonald. 1981. Library automation and library organization: An analysis of future trends. In *Options for the 80s: Proceedings of the Second National Conference of the Association of College and Research Libraries*, ed. Michael D. Kathman and Virgil F. Massman, 613–60. Greenwich, Conn.: JAI.

Information for a new age: Redefining the librarian. 1995. Chicago: Library Instruction Round Table, ALA.

Intner, Sheila S. 1993. *Interfaces: Relationships between library technical and public services*. Englewood, Colo.: Libraries Unlimited.

Intner, Sheila S. 1994. Technical services: An overview. In *Guide to technical services resources*, ed. Peggy Johnson, 5–26. Chicago: ALA.

Johnson, Peggy, and Sheila S. Intner, eds. 1994. *Recruiting, educating, and training librarians for collection development*. Westport, Conn.: Greenwood Pr.

Johnson-Laird, Philip N. 1983. *Mental models: Towards a cognitive science of language, inference, and consciousness*. Cambridge, Mass.: Harvard Univ. Pr.

Joyce, Patrick. 1987. The historical meanings of work: An introduction. In *The historical meanings of work*, ed. Patrick Joyce, 1–30. Cambridge, Eng.: Cambridge Univ. Pr.

Kanter, Rosabeth Moss. 1990. The new work force meets the changing workplace. In *The nature of work: Sociological perspectives*, ed. Kai Erikson and Steven Peter Vallas, 279–303. New Haven, Conn.: Yale Univ. Pr.

Katz, Robert, and Daniel Kahn. 1978. *The social psychology of organizations*. New York: Wiley.

Klaassen, David J. 1986. The provenance of archives under library administration: Organizational structures and organic relationships. *Journal of Library Administration* 7 (summer/fall): 35–47.

Kohn, Melvin L. 1990. Unresolved issues in the relationship between work and personality. In *The nature of work: Sociological perspectives*, ed. Kai Erikson and Steven Peter Vallas, 36–68. New Haven, Conn.: Yale Univ. Pr.

Kong, Leslie M., and R. A. H. Goodfellow. 1988. Charting a career path in the information professions. *College & Research Libraries* 49 (May): 207–16.

Krause, Elliott A. 1996. *Death of the guilds: Professions, states, and the advance of capitalism, 1930 to the present*. New Haven, Conn.: Yale Univ. Pr.

Lakoff, George, and Jack Johnson. 1980. *Metaphors we live by*. Chicago: Univ. of Chicago Pr.

Landy, Frank J., and Don A. Trumbo. 1976. *Psychology of work behavior*. Homewood, Ill.: Dorsey Pr.

Lave, Jean and Etienne Wenger. 1991. *Situated learning: Legitimate peripheral participation*. New York: Cambridge Univ. Pr. Referenced in Charles N. Darrah, *Learning and work: An exploration in industrial ethnography* (New York: Garland, 1996), 48.

Lawler, Edward E., III, and Douglas T. Hall. 1970. "Relationships of job characteristics to job involvement, satisfaction and intrinsic motivation." *Journal of Applied Psychology* 54 (4): 305–12.

Lawler, Edward E., III. 1992. *The ultimate advantage: Creating the high-involvement organization*. San Francisco: Jossey-Bass.

Le Goff, Jacques. 1980. *Time, work, and culture in the Middle Ages*. Chicago: Univ. of Chicago Pr.

Levine, Arthur. 1988. *Handbook on undergraduate curriculum*. San Francisco: Jossey-Bass.

Levine, John M., and Richard L. Moreland. 1989. Social values and multiple outcome comparisons. In *Social and moral values: Individual and societal perspectives*, ed. Nancy Eisenberg, Janusz Reykowski, and Ervin Staub, 195–212. Hillsdale, N.J.: Lawrence Erlbaum.

Lightfoot, Sara Lawrence. 1983. Afterward: The passion for portraiture. In *The good high school: Portraits of character and culture*, 369–378. New York: Basic Bks.

Littler, Craig R., ed. 1985. The future of work. In *The experience of work*, ed. Craig R. Littler, 277–80. Aldershot, Eng: Gower.

Littler, Craig R., ed. 1985. Introduction: The texture of work. In *The experience of work*, ed. Craig R. Littler, 1–9. Aldershot, Eng: Gower.

Lodahl, Thomas M., and Mathilde Kejner. 1965. The definition and measurement of job involvement. *Journal of Applied Psychology* 49 (1): 24–33.

Loe, Mary H. 1986. Thor tax ruling after 5 years: Its effect on publishing and libraries. *Library Acquisitions: Practice & Theory* 10 (3): 203–18.

Lortie, Dan C. 1975. *School-teacher: A sociological study*. Chicago: Univ. of Chicago Pr.

Lynch, Beverly P., and Jo Ann Verdin. 1983. Job satisfaction in libraries: Relationships of the work itself, age, sex, occupational group, tenure, supervisory level, career commitment, and library department. *Library Quarterly* 53 (4): 434–47.

Lynch, Beverly P., and Jo Ann Verdin. 1987. "Job satisfaction in libraries: A replication. *Library Quarterly* 57 (2): 190–202.

Maccoby, Michael. 1984. *Why work: Motivating and leading the new generation*. New York: Simon & Schuster.

Marshall, Catherine, and Gretchen B. Rossman. 1989. *Designing qualitative research*. Newbury Park, Calif.: Sage.

Marx, Karl. 1867/1967. *Capital: A critique of political economy*. New York: International Publishers.

Maslow, Abraham. 1954. *Motivation and personality*. New York: Harper & Row.

Massman, Virgil F. 1972. *Faculty status for librarians*. Metuchen, N.J.: Scarecrow.

McAnally, Arthur M., and Robert B. Downs. 1973. The changing role of directors of university libraries. *College & Research Libraries* 34 (Mar.): 103–25.

McGowan, Frank M. 1972. The association of research libraries, 1932–1962. (Ph.D. diss., Univ. of Pittsburgh).

McGregor, Douglas. 1960. *The human side of enterprise*. New York: McGraw-Hill.

McHenry, Dean E., and Associates. 1977. *Academic departments*. San Francisco: Jossey-Bass.

McHugh, Peter. 1968. *Defining the situation: The organization of meaning in social interaction*. Indianapolis: Bobbs-Merrill.

Mellon, Constance A. 1990. *Naturalistic inquiry for library science: Methods and applications for research, evaluation, and teaching.* Contributions in librarianship and information sciences, no. 64. Westport, Conn.: Greenwood.

Mendelsohn, Jennifer. 1995. Human help at OPAC terminals is user friendly: A preliminary study." *RQ* 34 (winter): 173–90.

Merikangas, Robert J. 1979. The academic reference librarian: Roles and development. In *New horizons for academic libraries: Papers presented at the First National Conference of the Association of College and Research Libraries, Boston, Massachusetts, November 8–11, 1978*, ed. Robert D. Stueart and Richard D. Johnson, 395–403. New York: K. G. Saur.

Merton, Robert K. 1982. *Social research and the practicing professions.* Cambridge, Mass.: Abt Bks.

Merton, Robert K., and Alice Kitt Rossi. 1968. Contributions to the theory of reference group behavior. In *Readings in reference group theory and research*, ed. Herbert H. Hyman and Eleanor Singer, 28–68. New York: Free Pr.

Millett, John D. 1962. *The academic community: An essay on organizations.* New York: McGraw–Hill.

Mills, C. Wright. 1951. "Work". In *White Collar: The American Middle Classes*, 215–38. New York: Oxford Univ. Pr.

Mohrman, Susan Albers, and Susan G. Cohen. 1995. When people get out of the box: New relationships, new systems. In *The changing nature of work*, ed. Ann Howard, 365–410. San Francisco: Jossey-Bass.

Moorhouse, H. F. 1987. The "work ethic" and "leisure" activity: The hot rod in post-war America. In *The historical meanings of work*, ed. Patrick Joyce, 237–57. Cambridge, Eng.: Cambridge Univ. Pr.

Moos, Rudolf H. 1986. Work as a human context. In *Psychology and work: Productivity, change, and employment*, eds. Robert Perloff and J. Richard Hackman, 5–52. Washington, D.C.: American Psychological Association.

Moran, Barbara B. 1989. The unintended revolution in academic libraries: 1939 to 1989 and beyond. *College & Research Libraries* 50 (Jan.): 25–41.

Morrison, Perry. 1969. *The career of the academic librarian: A study of the social origins, educational attainments, vocational experience, and per-*

sonality characteristics of a froup of American academic librarians. Chicago: ALA.

Mortimer, Jeylan T. 1979. *Changing attitudes toward work: Highlights of the literature.* Work & American Institute studies in productivity. New York: Pergamon.

Mortimer, Jeylan T., and Jon Lorence. 1979. Work experience and occupational value socialization: A longitudinal study. *American Journal of Sociology* 84 (6): 1361–85.

MOW International Research Team. 1987. *The meaning of working.* London: Academic Pr.

Musmann, Klaus. 1993. *Technological innovations in libraries, 1860–1960: An anecdotal history.* Westport, Conn.: Greenwood Pr.

Nord, Walter R., Arthur P. Brief, Jennifer M. Atieh, and Elizabeth M. Doherty. 1990. Studying meanings of work: The case for work values. In *Meanings of occupational work: A collection of essays*, ed. Arthur P. Brief and Walter R. Nord, 21–64. Lexington, Mass.: Lexington Bks.

Oberg, Larry R., Mark E. Mentges, P. N. McDermott, Vitoon Harusadangkul. 1992. The role, status, and working conditions of paraprofessionals: A national survey of academic libraries. *College & Research Libraries* 53 (May): 215–38.

Ogden, C. K., and I. A. Richards. 1946. *The meaning of meaning: A study of the influence of language upon thought and of the science of symbolism.* London: Kegan Paul, Trench, Trubner & Co.

O'Neil, Robert M. 1982. The university administrator's view of the university library. In *Priorities for academic libraries*, ed. Thomas J. Galvin and Beverly P. Lynch. Reprinted from *New Directions for Higher Education* 10 (Sept.): 5–12. San Francisco: Jossey-Bass.

Organisation for Economic Co-operation and Development, 1977. *Policies for life At work.* Paris: OECD.

Orzack, Louis H. 1959. Work as a "central life interest" of professionals. *Social Problems* 7 (fall): 125–32.

Osburn, Charles B. 1979. *Academic research and library resources: Changing patterns in America.* New Directions in Librarianship, no. 3. Westport, Conn.: Greenwood.

Osgood, Charles E. 1990. The nature and measurement of meaning. In *Language, meaning, and culture: The selected papers of C. E. Osgood,* ed. Charles E. Osgood and Oliver C. S. Tzeng. Centennial psychology series. New York: Praeger. Reprinted from *Psychological Bulletin*, 49 (1952): 197–237.

Ovitt, George Jr. 1987. *The restoration of perfection: Labor and technology in medieval culture.* New Brunswick, N.J.: Rutgers Univ. Pr.

Palmini, Cathleen C. 1994. The impact of computerization on library support staff: A study of support staff in academic libraries in Wisconsin. *College & Research Libraries* 55 (Mar.): 119–27.

Parmer, Coleen, and Dennis East. 1993. Job satisfaction among support staff in twelve Ohio academic libraries. *College & Research Libraries* 54 (Jan.): 43–57.

Patton, Michael Quinn. 1990. *Qualitative evaluation and research methods.* 2nd ed. Newbury Park, Calif.: Sage.

Powell, Ronald R., and Sheila D. Creth. 1986. Knowledge bases and library education. *College and Research Libraries* 47 (Jan.):16–27.

Qvale, Thoralf. 1988. On the dynamics of change. In *The meaning of work and technological options,* ed. Veronique de Keyser, Thoralf Qvale, Bernhard Wilpert, and S. Antonio Ruiz Quintanilla, 211–20. Chichester, Eng: Wiley.

Rabinowitz, S., and D. T. Hall. 1977. Organizational research on the job involvment. *Psychological Bulletin* 84: 265–88. Referenced in Loriann Roberson, Functions of work meanings in organizations: Work meanings and work motivation, 110. In *Meanings of occupational work: A collection of essays,* ed. Arthur P. Brief and Walter R. Nord, 107–34. Lexington, Mass.: Lexington Bks.

Radford, Marie L., and Gary P. Radford. 1997. Power, knowledge, and fear: Michel Foucault and the stereotype of the female librarian. *Library Quarterly* 67 (3): 250–66.

Ranganathan, S. R. 1970. Application to India. In *Sociological foundations of librarianship,* by Jesse Hauk Shera, 166–83. London: Asia Publishing.

Research universities and the national interest: A report from fifteen university presidents. 1977. New York: Ford Foundation.

Rice, Albert Kenneth. 1963. *The enterprise and its environment; A system theory of management organization.* London: Tavistock.

Roberson, Loriann. 1990. Functions of work meanings in organizations: work meanings and work motivation. In *Meanings of occupational work: A collection of essays*, ed. Arthur P. Brief and Walter R. Nord, 107–34. Lexington, Mass.: Lexington Bks.

Rodgers, Daniel T. 1978. *The work ethic in industrial America: 1850–1920*. Chicago: Univ. of Chicago Pr.

Rosenzweig, Robert M., and Barbara Turlington. 1982. *The research universities and their patrons*. Berkeley: Univ. of California Pr.

Ross, Lee, and Richard E. Nisbett. 1991. *The person and the situation: Perspectives of social psychology*. Philadelphia: Temple Univ. Pr.

Rosseel, Eric. 1986. The impact of changes in work ethics upon organizational life. In *The psychology of work and organization*, ed. G. Debus and H.-W. Schroiff, 291–99. Amsterdam: New Holland/Elsevier.

Rothstein, Samuel. 1955. *The development of reference services through academic traditions, public library practice and special librarianship*. ACRL monographs, no. 14. Chicago: ALA, ACRL.

Rothstein, Samuel. 1961. Reference service: The new dimension in librarianship. *College and Research Libraries* 22: 11–18.

Rousseau, Denise M., and Kimberly A. Wade-Benzoni. 1995. Changing individual-organization attachments: A two-way street. In *The changing nature of work*, ed. Ann Howard, 290–322. San Francisco: Jossey-Bass.

Rudolph, Frederick. 1962. *The American college and university: A history*. New York: A. Knopf.

Ruiz Quintanilla, S. Antonio. 1990. Major work meaning patterns toward a holistic picture. In *Work motivation*, ed. Uwe Kleinbeck, Hans-Henning Quast, Henk Thierry, and Hartmut Hacker, 257–72. Hillsdale, N.J.: Lawrence Erlbaum.

Ruiz Quintanilla, S. Antonio, and Bernhard Wilpert. 1988. The meaning of working—-Scientific status of a concept. In *The meaning of work and technological options*, ed. Veronique de Keyser, Thoralf Qvale, Bernhard Wilpert and S. Antonio Ruiz Quintanilla, 3–14. Chichester, Eng.: Wiley.

St. Clair, Jeffrey W., and Rao Aluri. 1977. Staffing the reference desk: Professionals or nonprofessionals? *Journal of Academic Librarianship* 3 (July): 149–53.

Salaman, Graeme. 1980. Organizations as constructors of social reality (II). In *Control and ideology in organizations*, ed. Graeme Salaman and Kenneth Thompson, 237–56. Milton Keynes, Eng.: Open Univ.

Pr.

Salomon, Kristine. 1988. The impact of CD-ROM on reference departments. *RQ* 28 (2): 203–15.

Samore, Theodore, and Doris C. Holladay. 1962. *Library statistics of colleges and universities, 1961–62: Institutional data.* Washington, D.C.: U.S. Department of Health, Education, and Welfare.

Sandelands, Lloyd E. 1988. Effects of work and play signals on task evaluation. *Journal of Applied Social Psychology* 18 (12): 1032–48.

Schatzman, Leonard, and Anselm L. Strauss. 1973. *Field research: Strategies for a natural sociology.* Englewood Cliffs, N.J.: Prentice-Hall.

Scherdin, Mary Jane, ed. 1994. *Discovering librarians: Profiles of a profession.* Chicago: ALA.

Schiller, Anita R. 1969. *Characteristics of professional personnel in college and university libraries.* Springfield, Ill.: Illinois State Library.

Sederberg, Peter C. 1984. *The politics of meaning: power and explanation in the construction of social reality.* Tucson, Ariz.: Univ. of Arizona Pr.

Senge, Peter M. 1990. *The fifth discipline: The art & practice of the learning organization.* New York: Doubleday/Currency.

Sergiovanni, Thomas J. 1994. Organizations or communities? Changing the metaphor changes the theory. *Educational Administration Quarterly* 30 (May): 214–26.

Shafritz, Jay M., and J. Steven Ott. 1991. *Classics of organization theory.* 3rd ed. Pacific Grove, Calif.: Brooks/Cole Publishing.

Shera, Jesse Hauk. 1970. *Sociological foundations of librarianship.* London: Asia Publishing.

Shiflett, Orvin Lee. 1981. *Origins of American academic librarianship.* Norwood, N.J.: Ablex.

Shirk, Evelyn. 1965. *The ethical dimension: An approach to the philosophy of values and valuing.* New York: Appleton-Century-Crofts.

Shores, Louis. 1966. *Origins of the American college library, 1638–1800.* Hamden, Conn.: Shoe String Pr.

Singleton, W. T. 1989. *The mind at work: Psychological ergonomics.* Cambridge, Eng.: Cambridge Univ. Pr.

Smith, Adam. 1789/1937. *An inquiry into the nature and causes of the wealth of nations.* New York: The Modern Library. Referenced in Herbert Applebaum, *The concept of work: Ancient, medieval, and modern.* SUNY series in the anthropology of work. (Albany, N.Y.: State

Univ. of New York Pr.), 393.

Spradley, James P. 1979. *The ethnographic interview*. New York: Holt, Rinehart and Winston.

Statistical abstract of the United States, 1992. 112th ed. Washington, D.C.: U. S. Department of Commerce.

Stewart, Phyllis L., and Muriel G. Cantor. 1974. *Varieties of work experience: The social control of occupational groups and roles*. New York: Wiley.

Strauss, Anselm. 1959. *Mirrors and masks: The search for identity*. Glencoe, Ill.: Free Pr.

Strauss, Anselm. 1987. *Qualitative analysis for social scientists*. Cambridge, Eng.: Cambridge Univ. Pr. Referenced in Lee Braude, *Work and workers: A sociological analysis* (Malabar, Fla.: Robert E. Krieger), 158–59.

Strauss, Anselm, and Juliet Corbin. 1990. *Basics of qualitative research: Grounded theory procedures and techniques*. Newbury Park, Calif.: Sage.

Taylor, Steven J., and Robert Bogdan. 1984. *Introduction to qualitative research methods: The search for meanings*. New York: Wiley.

Thompson, Kenneth. 1980. Organizations as constructors of social reality (I). In *Control and ideology in organizations*, ed. Graeme Salaman and Kenneth Thompson, 216–36. Milton Keynes, Eng.: Open Univ. Pr.

Tiefel, Virginia. 1995. Education for the academic library user in the year 2000. In *Information for a new age: Redefining the librarian*, 57–77. Chicago: Library Instruction Round Table, ALA.

Tilgher, Adriano. 1930/1958. *Homo faber: Work through the ages*. Trans. Dorothy Canfield Fisher. Chicago: Regnery.

Tornatzky, Louis G. 1986. Technological change and the structure of work. In *Psychology and work: Productivity, change, and employment*, ed. Robert Perloff and J. Richard Hackman, 53–83. Washington, D.C.: American Psychological Association.

Trice, Harrison M. 1993. *Occupational subcultures in the workplace*. Cornell Studies in Industrial and Labor Relations, no. 26. Ithaca, N.Y.: ILR Pr.

Tucker, John Mark. 1979. The origins of bibliographic instruction in academic libraries, 1876–1914. In *New horizons for academic libraries: Papers presented at the First National Conference of the Association of College and Research Libraries, Boston, Massachusetts, November 8–11, 1978*, ed. Robert D. Stueart and Richard D. Johnson, 268–76. New

York: K. G. Saur.

Tuttle, Helen W. 1976. From cutter to computer: Technical services in academic and research libraries, 1876–1976. In *Libraries for teaching, libraries for research: Essays for a century*, ed. Richard D. Johnson. ACRL Publications in Librarianship, no. 39: 71–97. Chicago: ALA. Reprinted from *College & Research Libraries* 37 (Sept. 1976): 421–51.

Vallas, Steven Peter. 1990. Comments and observations on the nature of work."In *The nature of work: Sociological perspectives*, ed. Kai Erikson and Steven Peter Vallas, 343–62. New Haven, Conn.: Yale Univ. Pr.

Vander Zanden, James Wilfrid. 1987. *Social psychology*. 4th ed. New York: Random House.

Veysey, Laurence R. 1965. *The emergence of the American university*. Chicago: Univ. of Chicago Pr.

Vroom, Victor H. 1995. *Work and motivation*. San Francisco: Jossey-Bass. Originally published by Wiley, 1964.

Walters, Raymond. 1921. Statistics of registration of thirty American universities for 1920. *School and society* 13, no. 318 (Jan. 29): 121–28.

Walters, Raymond. 1940. Statistics of registration in American universities and colleges, 1940. *School and society* 52, no. 1355 (Dec. 14): 601–19.

Weber, David C. 1976. A century of cooperative programs among academic libraries. In *Libraries for teaching, libraries for research: Essays for a century*, ed. Richard D. Johnson. ACRL publications in librarianship, no. 39: 185–201. Chicago: ALA. Reprinted from *College & Research Libraries* 37 (May 1976): 205–21.

Weber, Max. 1930. *The protestant ethic and the spirit of capitalism*, trans. T. Parsons. New York: Charles Scribner's Sons.

Weick, Karl E. 1976. Educational organizations as loosely coupled systems. *Administrative Science Quarterly* 21 (Mar.): 1–19.

Whitbeck, George Walter. 1970. The influence of librarians in liberal arts colleges as demonstrated by their role in selected areas of decision making. (Ph.D. diss., Rutgers Univ).

Wiegand, Wayne A. 1984. View from the top: The library administrator's changing perspective on standardization schemes and cataloging practices in American libraries, 1891–1901. In *Reference services and technical services: Interactions in library practice*, ed. Gordon Stevenson and Sally Stevenson. *The Reference Librarian* 9: 11–27. New York: Haworth.

Wilson, Pauline. 1982. *Stereotype and status: Librarians in the United States.* Westport, Conn.: Greenwood.

Wirth, Arthur G. 1992. *Education and sork for the year 2000: Choices we face.* San Francisco: Jossey-Bass.

Works, George Alan. 1927. *College and university library problems: A study of a selected group of institutions prepared for the Association of American Universities.* Chicago: ALA.

Zuboff, Shoshana. 1988. *In the age of the smart machine: The future of work and power.* New York: Basic Bks.

Index

DISCARD

DISCARD

DATE DUE

GAYLORD			PRINTED IN U.S.A.